# THE LITTLE BOOK OF BOARDS

A BOARD MEMBER'S HANDBOOK FOR SMALL
(AND VERY SMALL) NONPROFITS

ERIK HANBERG

# CONTENTS

# ONE

# INTRODUCTION

FOR A SMALL (OR very small) nonprofit, there may be nothing as important to its mission or overall success as the quality of its board.

The point might be best made by contrasting the small nonprofit board with the board of a large—or enormous—nonprofit. Board members of a billion-dollar hospital likely can't know the name of every doctor or nurse in the hospital's huge workforce. They likely haven't set foot in every room of the vast institution, haven't evaluated every single contract line-by-line. They rely on the executive director or CEO to administer policies on their behalf.

For an organization such as this, the quality of the board will only partly affect the health of the overall nonprofit. Would a board making consistently bad and irresponsible decisions affect the hospital's viability? Yes, of course. Would a merely mildly ineffective board damage the overall health? Probably not noticeably. There's just too much inertia and institutional knowledge to counteract a board's minor neglect.

This is not the case at a small or very small nonprofit.

Board members at small nonprofits are often highly engaged in the work of the organization, often by necessity. They may even be essential to its work and continued operation, making up the core of a group of volunteers and doing the actual work of the nonprofit. Board members of small nonprofits often know every tiny detail about the organization—after all, it's a small nonprofit, so maybe there's just not all that much to know.

Because of this, a board that is just "mildly ineffective" likely means that the entire organization is "mildly ineffective." Or worse. The board's decisions are amplified, affecting the entire organization and the success (or failure) of its mission very quickly.

On the other hand, the board of a small nonprofit that understands its role, that is focused on the right tasks, and is committed to improvement will create an organization that is bigger than the sum of its parts.

Reaching this place, though, can be hard for a small nonprofit. Small nonprofits often have—frankly—very "green" boards. A majority of board members on a small nonprofit board may never have served on a board before. Whereas by the time you get invited to join the board of a hospital, you have probably served on dozens of boards.

The depth of experience at a small nonprofit is just not as deep.

This slim handbook is designed to be the tool those board members need to understand the roles and responsibilities of being on a board of directors—especially the board of directors of a small nonprofit. It's intentionally short so that you can get what you need and then get back to the business of your board.

This book is broken up into the three main sections:

The first, and largest, part is written expressly for the new board member who has just joined a board. What does a board do? What is your job? What will your first meetings be like?

What questions should you ask? Even veteran board members may find this part to be a good refresher.

The second part covers the specific responsibilities and roles of board leadership—primarily president (or chair) and also the common positions of president-elect, past president, treasurer, secretary, and committee chair. It should be helpful to someone stepping into the office for the first time, as well as a new board member who is looking for clarity on responsibilities of the officers on the board.

The third and final part of the book is the appendix, which covers recommendations on bylaws, recruiting, and committee structure, as well as an overview of Robert's Rules of Order.

Throughout all sections, you will discover useful tips and practical suggestions written specifically for the small nonprofit. That means that I might spell out an "ideal" solution but also give some alternative suggestions on how they might work in practice.

How big is a small (or very small) nonprofit?

As a working definition, a small nonprofit has a budget of less than $1 to $1.5 million and fewer than 15 people on staff. A very small nonprofit has a budget of less than $250,000 and (at most) one or two staff members.

There is another kind of board member who should find this book helpful: one who sits on the board of a young nonprofit. Everything is new on the board of a young nonprofit —there aren't cultures or years of policies to rely on. So even if your nonprofit is bigger than what I define as a "small" nonprofit, there should be a lot here for you as well.

## My story

I always believe it's important to share my own story before we delve into the meat of the book.

I got my start in nonprofits early. My first job out of college was for a nonprofit and it's been nonprofits ever since. Whether in positions of marketing, development (fundraising), or administration—I've been the director of two nonprofits—my heart is with the great work that nonprofits do.

My first real contact with a board of directors was at the age of twenty-three, when a board hired me as the director of a nonprofit movie theater—something of a dream job for a film buff like me.

I still remember that final interview in front of a board of seventeen people. It almost felt like a firing squad, with questions coming from all sides. But I was hired!

At the time, the theater was only six years old, and many of the people on the board were founding members of the nonprofit. In the early days, that first board had been essential to keeping the lights on and the popcorn popping. But with a renewed interest in independent cinema from the community, the theater was doing much better financially, leading to a time of real questioning for the board. If they weren't sweeping up the theater, what was their job? They had to weigh the overall direction of the organization ("Are we 'just' a movie theater, or are we something more?"); learn about fundraising (and step forward to make the first donations); and figure out their role in a new landscape.

In retrospect, I had some opinions about the board's decisions and pushed them pretty strongly in the direction I favored. I was young, just two years out of college, and it was still a shock to me that not everyone would agree with what I thought were clearly very good ideas. I learned a lot through that experience about listening and working with a group of people who had a shared vision but different ideas on how to get there.

The job did put me into a more visible place in my hometown of Tacoma, Washington, and after I got the job, I found that I started to be invited onto boards. Both my parents had volunteered on boards when I was growing up, so I was excited that it was "my turn." I thought it would be prestigious somehow, so I agreed to sit on a few boards, sight unseen.

So it came as a surprise when after less than a year on one board, I discovered that the organization was never actually issued a check for a key grant it had been awarded—yet the nonprofit still provided the service anyway. There was now a huge loss on the books and I—as a board member—would be personally liable if we didn't find the money. *What?* No one told me that board members were liable!

Since then, I'm happy to say that I've served on more than a dozen boards, committees, and advisory groups. I've been in all sorts of roles—from the new guy who doesn't know anyone, to the old hand who explains to new board members how things work.

I even had an uncommon experience in the world of nonprofits—while I was serving as president of the board of one nonprofit, that board decided to enter into talks to merge with another nonprofit, combining their missions, staff, and resources. But that wasn't enough of a hurdle: the merger had a fixed deadline, so that funding sources could be correctly transferred. *And* we had to get the approval of three elected bodies, comprising a total of nineteen individually elected officials. What should have been a relatively easy year as president turned into a major endeavor of handholding, special planning meetings, and very long phone calls. But we did it! And the merger has stuck.

All that diverse nonprofit and board experience ended up coming in handy when I was elected to the board of Metro Parks Tacoma, a junior municipal agency with an annual budget of more than $40 million. Our board of five commissioners sets policy, represents the public interest, and supervises the executive director in the operations of the park district, which comprises more than ninety parks, several beaches and pools, and even two zoos. An elected board overseeing a public agency has several key differences with a nonprofit, but many of the principles of how a board interacts with staff and the overall mission stay the same. My experience there over the last five years has further clarified just where a small nonprofit should emulate a big board—and where it shouldn't.

I hope that all my experience, from organizations large and small, will be useful as you get ready to join a board of directors.

Meet Dennis

In my experience, stories are always more compelling than lectures. With that in mind, my previous books for small (and very small) nonprofits told the story of Linda, the executive director of the Smallville Historical Society. We followed Linda's initial work to get a handle on her nonprofit (*The Little Book of Nonprofit Leadership*), her journey into fundraising (*The Little Book of Gold*), and embrace of marketing and social media (*The Little Book of Likes*).

Linda will make a cameo in this book, but we're going to follow someone else instead.

Meet Dennis.

Dennis is a retired plumber. Not one to let grass grow under his feet, after he retired he soon started volunteering at the pioneer cabin operated by the Historical Society. Dennis discovered a new joy he never would have imagined when he was younger—dressing up in period costume and giving presentations to school tours about Smallville's pioneer days.

When he got a fundraising letter from Linda asking for support, he happily gave $250 to the organization he liked so much. He didn't know at the time that it was a gift larger than many Historical Society board members had given. And he didn't know that Linda immediately started to think of him as a possible candidate for the board.

The next time someone stepped down from the board, Linda emailed her board president and suggested he meet with Dennis to talk about the possibility of joining the board. Dennis agreed to meet, though he was reluctant. He'd never thought of himself as someone who would be in a "boardroom."

His first question to the board president might be familiar to many of you.

*"Just what does a board of directors do?"*

# PART ONE

# HOW TO BE A BOARD MEMBER

# WHAT DOES A BOARD DO?

"JUST WHAT DOES a board of directors do?" Dennis asked the board president.

It's a simple question, but there's no simple answer. The board of a hospital does different things than the board of a soup kitchen. The board of a nonprofit going through a capital campaign does different things than a board looking for a new executive director.

But while the activities might be different, the core responsibilities of a board member remain fairly common throughout all nonprofits.

The board president nodded at Dennis's question, appreciating that he was willing to be candid about what he did and did not know. "We do a lot, but it may not be in the ways that you think. In fact, our first and most important job may surprise you. We make sure the nonprofit is following its mission."

Ensure the nonprofit is following its mission

Dennis looked at the board president blankly. "Isn't that pretty obvious? The Historical Society promotes Smallville history... and stuff."

"Right," the president smiled. "It's the 'and stuff' that gets tricky. Specifically, our mission is 'to preserve, protect, and promote the history of Smallville.'"

"Seems clear enough," Dennis said.

"So let's say there was a grant available for forty thousand dollars that could only be used to talk about arts in Smallville. Should we apply for it?"

"That's a lot of money, obviously, but I guess not."

"Not an easy choice, is it? We'd certainly want to check if there were a way to use it to tell the story of arts in the history of Smallville. Or maybe they include cultural nonprofits with arts organizations. But if we couldn't use those 'lenses,' you're right. We shouldn't apply for it."

Making sure your nonprofit is following its mission might sound obvious—like checking whether the symphony is performing symphonies. But keep in mind that a mission is more than just a nice idea. It's the legal reason for your existence. It's something that the Internal Revenue Service actually cares about. The board is responsible for making sure the mission is followed.

Why is this a big deal? Because the mission is what grants your nonprofit its tax-exempt status. *If there were no mission, you would be just a regular business and you would be taxed accordingly.*

Let's say your nonprofit's mission was to "save the whales," and you sold T-shirts with a message on the front that said "Save the Whales." That's not enough on its own to make you a nonprofit. Unless you are actually giving money to whale conservation or are otherwise educating the public about whales, the IRS could audit your organization and charge you for tax fraud—operating a T-shirt business in the guise of a nonprofit.

More commonly, this duty for board members comes up when a staff member or a board member suggests a new program to be offered by a nonprofit. The first thought of a board member should be: is this part of our mission? Sometimes this cuts the other way, too. The Smallville Historical Society primarily operates a pioneer cabin. But its mission says nothing about focusing on just the pioneer days. There have been 150 years of history since then! A board member at a nonprofit needs to be ready to consider new ways of living its mission. Maybe it would surprise Dennis if the Historical Society created an exhibit on the tumultuous labor relations that hit the town in the 1920s, but it's just as much "on mission" as the pioneer cabin is.

(Note: Nonprofits can have some non-mission-related income streams. For example, a theater can rent out its auditorium to a corporate meeting to generate earned income. Your nonprofit should consult a tax attorney, or confirm during an annual audit whether there is any tax liability for income that may not be strictly "on mission." Raising the question is an important duty of a board or individual board member.)

### Set policy

"Our next big role is in setting policy," continued the board president. "I know it sounds boring. But it's vitally important to making sure that the nonprofit is on the right path."

"Can you give me an example?" Dennis asked.

"Well, two board meetings ago, we passed a comprehensive marketing plan. That's a form of policy. And last meeting we passed an environmental stewardship policy. So we make efforts to use pitchers of water at events instead of water bottles, and biodegradable forks and knives."

"That seems like it's not really related to history," Dennis said.

"It doesn't have to be. Policy is about *how* we fulfill our mission—all aspects of it. It can cover personnel, finances, board operations, and more."

"What other polices do you have?"

"Many. We don't store customer credit card numbers. Employees working more than 30 hours per week may opt into our retirement plan. Partner organizations must be approved by the board of directors. Policies create a framework for how we operate, one that Linda has to work within."

Please note, there is a tendency of boards to start creating policy around something it doesn't like, no matter how minor. "Casual Fridays are not allowed" is the kind of policy created after a Casual Friday gone wrong. Generally speaking, the temptation to create a narrow policy like this is counterproductive. How big is your board? Seven? Seventeen? Is it really a good use of time at a board meeting for so many people to talk about creating a new policy around Casual Fridays? Or is it easier for the board president to pull the executive director aside and ask her to deal with it as a supervisor?

Setting policy is an important function of a board, so long as it doesn't try to use policy to overly prescribe the actions of the executive director or staff carrying it out.


Ensure the financial health of the nonprofit

"The other way we direct how the nonprofit runs is through the creation of an annual budget," the president said. "We as a board have a responsibility to keep an eye on the finances. So we establish what we're going to do every year with a budget, and then we get reports on it from the treasurer at every board meeting."

"I haven't spent a lot of time with big budgets and stuff," Dennis said.

"The budget isn't that big," the board president said with a smile. "Although hopefully it will be someday. But really, don't worry about it. We will take you through orientation before you officially join the board. And there's always a learning curve. It's not a problem at all. As long as you're willing to ask questions and do your best."

"I can do that."

"It's worth pointing out here, too, that—technically speaking —the most we as a board get to weigh in on the daily operation of the nonprofit is through the budget. It's the job of the executive director to carry out our budget, within the guidelines of policy and the mission. She reports how we're doing at board and committee meetings, by providing written reports, and—of course—financial reports. But we don't really get to tell her how to run day-to-day operations."

"I get that."

The board president smiled. "I know, it all makes sense *in theory*. And we'll talk more about that in a second. For now, though, just know that the budget is the main way we set operations for the year."

One specific means of financial oversight: an audit

Beyond budget and regular financial reports, there is one more part to ensuring a nonprofit's financial health. It's the job of confirming that what the treasurer and the executive director are reporting to the board is accurate. This is accomplished through a regularly scheduled audit of a nonprofit's financials.

The way this works is that a board will hire an accounting firm to review the books and look for any anomalies. They aren't just looking for malfeasance such as embezzlement, but also simply looking for ways that a nonprofit can improve. Some audits will return recommendations for financial policies; others will just point out a systems flaw or a *potential* for malfeasance and leave it to the board to decide how to take action to address it.

Some nonprofits are required to perform an audit depending on their size, state law, or whether they receive government grants. If you are required to do this, your fellow board members are likely aware of this. As you learn about the nonprofit, it's worth asking about.

For a small (or very) small nonprofit, the cost of an audit might be too onerous to manage. Know that there is a range of costs and that they can vary widely depending on the accounting firm, so look around.

An alternative to the cost of an audit is something called a financial "review," which can be much cheaper. At one small nonprofit I worked at, the board performed a full audit every third year and a review in the other two years to keep the cost down.

Whether it's a review or an audit, remember that this is a procedure the board itself should be managing, *not* the executive director. A board should expect full compliance from the executive director and staff, but this is a job for the board. Often this task falls to the treasurer by default and is handled by the finance committee. In actuality, it would be even better if a separate committee managed the audit process, to protect against the outside chance that your treasurer is part of some malfeasance or is performing poorly.

Interlude

Whether enormous or very small, those three board responsibilities—mission, policy, and financial oversight—will create a functioning nonprofit. Every board, no matter the size, has these three responsibilities. That doesn't mean that the duties we'll cover later are optional, but rather that these three form a particular legal and fiduciary core of responsibilities for governance.

Think about it this way: the first task of a board is ensuring that a nonprofit is on mission. The next task is setting general policy for how that mission is carried out. The next task is ensuring that it has the financial resources to do so.

With those three things established—mission, policy, and budget—an executive director should be able to carry out the vast majority of the daily business of a nonprofit on behalf of the board.

Fundraising

Not all nonprofits need to fundraise. Perhaps they rely on large grants or contracts, or earned revenue, or perhaps the nonprofit is so small that the band of volunteers doesn't need to raise money for what they do.

But most nonprofits do fundraise, and the board should be at the center of those efforts. It's an extension of the board's financial oversight responsibility. If your nonprofit is asking for donations from others, then your board members have a duty to give, and there should be no exceptions. The norm should be 100 percent giving. For a plan to get there, if you aren't already, I recommend my book *The Little Book of Gold: Fundraising for Small (and Very Small) Nonprofits*.

I like to say that for individual board members, this means giving a gift that is "significant" to them. Another way to phrase this is to say that whatever giving you do to other charitable organizations, one of your biggest three financial gifts of the year (by total dollar amount) should be to the nonprofit on whose board you serve. Some board members give a smaller monthly amount if they can't afford to write a single check once a year.

Some nonprofits say "give it or get it," to mean that if you don't have the resources to give yourself, you are obligated to raise it from others. But that's not the full story. It's not an either/or. You should be doing both.

What that entails varies by nonprofit.

During his meeting with Dennis about joining the board of the Smallville Historical Society, the board president laid out the fundraising responsibilities expected of a board member.

"We do have an expectation of 100 percent board giving," the president said.

"Is there a specific amount I'm expected to donate?" Dennis asked. (Some nonprofits *do* have a number. It's important to know these expectations before you join!)

"We don't set a number," the board president said. "But you should know that the average gift from the board is $175. It's been rising slowly for the past couple of years, which we're very proud of. We ask board members to give a stretch gift that is significant for them. The amount is treated confidentially, as it is for all donors. Only the executive director and I know the exact figure any single board member donates."

The board president continued, "We also expect our board members to call donors who give more than $50 and thank them for their donation. That usually means a handful of calls per board member. And we ask that you attend our annual fundraising breakfast and fill a table with your friends. That's it!"

That is a *very* reasonable expectation for a board member of a small nonprofit. It's focused, and it doesn't waste the board member's time trying to sell raffle tickets or other high-energy, low-yield activities that can often sap a board member's energy and divert them from their other, more important duties.

Your board might have slightly different expectations, such as setting up a meeting with a friend who is being cultivated as a donor, and possibly attending that meeting with the board president or executive director. Some boards may look to you to make an "ask" yourself. If that's the case, you should ask for training or read the first part of *The Little Book of Gold: Fundraising for Small (and Very Small) Nonprofits*, which covers the process.

### A note on "working boards"

Sometimes a nonprofit board member will tell you that their board is a "working board" and not a "fundraising board." I should tell you now: this is a false distinction.

Sure, the board members of the Metropolitan Museum of Art in New York City spend huge amounts of time fundraising for the organization. If that's not a "fundraising board" I don't know what is. But you don't have to be expected to raise millions of dollars at swanky parties in order to fundraise for the nonprofit.

Anyone who chooses to serve on a nonprofit board should be expected to give personally, and to give generously (whatever that means to them).

You can be both a working board *and* a fundraising board.

### Strategic planning and visioning

"There's another important part to our work, and it's actually one we're in the thick of right now," the board president continued. "Strategic planning. We have a budget for the next year, but it's our job as a board to look ahead longer than that. Five years, maybe even twenty years. We need to know where we want to go so that every year we can make a little bit of progress in that direction."

"Can you really plan twenty years out?" Dennis asked. "A lot could change between then and now."

"A lot almost certainly *will* change. We expect that. But there are some things we can probably make reasonable assumptions about, too. For example, we have a contract with the state to operate the pioneer cabin on their behalf. We know the state budget always seems to be tight—and might keep getting tighter. So we want to make sure we develop some alternate ways of running the cabin without that contract if we ever need to. That's one part of the strategic plan. We also want to expand our programming outside the cabin.

"Operating the cabin is not the only thing we do, though people think it is. So what if—God forbid—something terrible happened to the cabin? A tornado scooped it away or something. Would our nonprofit cease to operate because the cabin was gone? We want to make sure that our tours to schools and other events are strong so that we have something to fall back on. So we're working on strengthening those as well. That's less about 'visioning' and more about making sure we're not at risk. But both get to the same thing: thinking about the nonprofit over the long term."

"That sounds kind of fun."

"It is. But it's hard, too. People have different values and ideas and we're trying to reconcile those. And it's easy to get caught up in monthly reports and the budget. But I've worked really hard to make sure we have time on the agenda this year for the strategic plan. I think it will really pay off."

A strategic plan is often called a "long-range" plan or a

"twenty-year" plan, or any number of other similar names that gets to the same idea. No matter the name, the plan needs to ask the big-picture questions:

*Is our "market" changing? Is the nature of the population we serve changing? Are funders changing how they see our work? How is technology changing how we might do business? Could we widen, or narrow, our mission and have a greater impact? How much money should we have in the bank?*

Strategic planning is an extension of a board's three responsibilities of mission, policy, and financial oversight. It's taking that work and projecting it out into the future in such a way that an organization can try to prevent being caught unaware by a significant change. Too many nonprofits find themselves in a place where their funding has been cut off because they didn't diversify it, or the need they serve has changed enough that they are no longer equipped to fill it.

Despite the importance of strategic planning, it is a task often skipped by small nonprofit boards. Retreats are hard to schedule, and regular business at board meetings feels too pressing, so it gets put on the backburner. Later in the book are some tips to free up time at a board meeting, but for now, know that strategic planning should be a key priority for a nonprofit board. If a board isn't busy developing a strategic plan, it should be occupied evaluating how it is doing at implementing the plan.

One note I think is worth lingering on: The process of strategic planning often relies on a good relationship between the board and an executive director. Mutual trust is important, because many of the answers to the important questions of the plan will, by necessity, come from the executive director and staff. An executive director, simply by living the work of a nonprofit on a daily basis, will often have the best knowledge the board will need to create a plan.

That implies trust from the board that the executive director knows her job, knows her work, and isn't trying to shoehorn the board down a path that it doesn't want to travel. It also implies trust from the executive director that the board has the best interest of the nonprofit at heart, that it respects the director's judgment and knowledge, and also that the board has wisdom and ideas that need to be addressed and considered—and not just written off. In short, mutual trust. It's a much harder process when this isn't present.

"To hire and fire the executive director"

"Our next major duty as a board is to 'hire and fire' the executive director," the board president said. "But the truth is that the only reason people say it like that is because it rhymes. Hire, supervise, evaluate, and terminate the employment of the executive director just doesn't have the same ring, even though it's much more accurate."

"What exactly does that mean for me?" Dennis asked. Just bringing up the word "fire" made him uncomfortable. He *liked* Linda.

"Honestly, it shouldn't mean a lot. Linda is doing a great job and the nonprofit is really firing on all cylinders these days. But there are some important things to talk about.

"The first is that it's important to understand that Linda works for the board as a whole, not for any particular board member. We all can't treat her like our personal employee, otherwise she would spend so much time doing things for thirteen board members that she wouldn't have any time to actually run the nonprofit. That means that you shouldn't email her and ask her to create a new report about the costs and benefits of a new program. Frankly, no single board member should get to do that... except maybe me," the board president said.

"Let's say that hypothetically that I *did* want to see a

cost/benefit report of a new program?" Dennis asked. "Maybe I thought it was important to my duty to the finances or something. What should I do if I can't ask Linda?"

"You should ask the treasurer or the finance committee as a whole to look at the issue. Maybe they think the report would be useful and then they ask Linda to create it. Maybe the treasurer knows the figures off the top of his head and could give you a run-down of it in a five-minute conversation. But it stays within the chain of command. We work through committees. So committees can assign work to Linda, but not an individual. It prevents someone from assigning extra work to Linda and bogging her down. But it also makes sure that other board members are in the loop. We don't want everyone acting on their own initiative without telling anyone else what they're doing—it would just get too crazy. Committees keep that from happening. Our work supervising Linda and giving her direction should happen exclusively at the board or committee level and not one-on-one between an individual board member and her. Again, the exception to that is me as the board president, and even then I'm channeling what I hear from the board, not pushing my own agenda."

Interlude: Assigning work to Linda vs. using the committee structure

A lot of people profess not to like committees and view them as a waste of time. This is especially true for people who are not familiar with the sometimes messy and frustrating work of a board and its committees.

To that end, I'd like to give a scenario that a good board committee structure is designed to prevent and explain why you, an individual board member, should work within the board committee structure as much as possible—and not just ask your executive director to do something.

Let's imagine a scenario in which Dennis has just joined the board of the Historical Society. Toward the end of his first board meeting he suggested an idea that he'd been thinking about for some time. Namely, that the Historical Society should send historical re-enactors out into the community and then film them interacting with modern-day objects with confusion, maybe breaking things they don't understand. He described how he thought a series of six or eight guerrilla-style videos would go viral on the Internet, how people would love watching the funny reaction shots of shop owners.

Many of the board members laughed and there was a general nodding of heads. The board president looked to the executive director and said, "Linda, can you look into Dennis's idea a bit more?" Linda nodded, and the board meeting wrapped up.

When Linda came into work the next day, she looked at her notes and wasn't sure where to go. It was an interesting idea, but she was trying to figure out how to get her head around it. The Smallville Historical Society didn't have any video cameras, and the last time it had hired out video work for a very short promotional video at its fundraiser, it had cost several hundred dollars. Now the nonprofit was supposed to create as many as six or eight videos? Filmed with a secret camera or something? Could the volunteer historical re-enactors act well enough to do it? Were the other people in the video supposed to be in on it? What kind of waivers and documents would they need? Were the volunteers *actually* supposed to break things?

She liked the idea, but it seemed incredibly expensive and time-consuming to pull off well. What should she do, she wondered? Should she create a budget and present it to Dennis to show him how much it would cost? What if she just ignored it and hoped no one followed up?

(This situation is all too common. An idea comes up from a board member—good or bad—and it gets referred to the executive director to "look into." Now she's stuck trying to figure out what to do with it. There's no budget, there's no time to implement it, but there's a board member who has a personal investment in seeing it happen—a board member, we should remember, who helps make employment decisions about the executive director. This dynamic can create a difficult situation that is almost guaranteed to create frustration or resentment.)

Linda called her board president and explained her situation. He suggested she sit down with Dennis and explain things. Linda took his advice, but when she met with Dennis over coffee, he kept suggesting ways that it could happen. Some were workable, but there was still the central issue for Linda: where would the money come from and who had the time and expertise to coordinate the project and make sure it turned out well?

After the coffee meeting, Dennis called the board president to complain that Linda was stonewalling a good idea. They spent a half hour on the phone until the board president agreed to put it on the agenda at the next board meeting. Now Linda and Dennis were upset at each other, and the board president just wanted the whole thing to go away.

At the board meeting, the entire board spent twenty minutes talking about the idea and how to pay for it. Whereas the meeting before had a lot of heads nodding in agreement, this one was contentious, because there were actual costs associated with the idea. Finally someone made a motion that any money raised above the budgeted revenue at the annual fundraiser would be dedicated to go toward this project. It was a 5–3 vote in favor of the idea, the first split vote that Linda could remember in some time.

This scenario paints a picture of a board that has forgotten its key responsibilities. It has determined a specific project of operations, it has earmarked spending for special projects outside of the budget process, and it has needlessly allowed for a rift between board members and between at least one board member and the executive director.

I know it seems crazy that something as boring-sounding as a committee of the board could have prevented this, but it's true. Here's how:

*First, a good committee structure will harness the experience and wisdom of board members into the key areas where the nonprofit really needs it.*

Board members *want* to contribute their experience and wisdom. They won't volunteer their time if they don't feel that they're helping. Committees give board members a way to contribute to work that needs to be done.

*Second, it does so without allowing a "lone wolf" to establish his or her own agenda without input from other board members.*

Like Dennis, a board member passionate about a particular topic can often push a board strongly enough that factions or "sides" develop. Boards get enormous benefits from having a diverse set of people in the room. But as soon as they stop working collaboratively and collegially, a lot of those benefits go away. People stop listening to each other and start dismissing each other's opinions, and board meetings start to feel tense.

. . .

*Third, a good committee structure allows for experts to emerge on the board.*

Not everyone can be an expert in everything. A governance committee will spend more time with the bylaws than the full board. A finance committee will spend more time with the balance sheet than the full board. This is not about a board outsourcing its responsibilities to a committee. But a board can rely on a small group to study an issue or a particular facet of the organization in-depth.

*Fourth, a good committee structure respects the time of the board.*

The formalized structure and clear expectations (such as attend board meetings and sit on one committee) help board members understand what's expected of them, and prevent a nonprofit board from continuing to ask for more, more, more from its members.

*And finally, committees allow a small group to consider new and possibly controversial ideas in a relatively free environment that might have been immediately nixed by the full board.*

Let's say a board was considering implementing term limits, something that might make the long-serving members of the board anxious. A governance committee is likely to have more opportunity to fully consider all the pros and cons of the idea at its meeting than at a full board meeting, when some board members start to feel unwelcome by their fellow board members. By "opportunity," I mean the committee has more time (a governance committee could devote a full hour to the topic, whereas a board might be able to allot only 15 minutes) and also more freedom (it's easier to hear a wide range of ideas in a small group, especially when there's not a chance of an immediate vote for something to become policy).


Let's tell a different story about Dennis and his idea. This time, the Smallville Historical Society has a better committee structure in place.

Just as before, when he finished describing his idea for a series of guerrilla-style videos of costumed re-enactors, many of the board members laughed, and there was a general nodding of heads. But this time, the board president looked to the chair of the marketing committee and said, "Can the marketing committee look into Dennis's idea and report back in a month or two?" The committee chair nodded, and the board meeting wrapped up.

Before the next meeting, the chair of the committee called Dennis and got more information about his idea. He was debating whether to invite Dennis to the committee meeting, and finally decided to invite him.

At the next marketing committee meeting, Dennis shared his idea again, and the group began talking about all the things you could do with it. In her role as the executive director, Linda was in attendance at the meeting. Although she tried to hold back her opinions, she finally couldn't help it, and she shared her worries about how much it would cost. She told them about the three companies she got bids from for the promotional video and the range of costs, which were all fairly high.

The discussion began to focus on the means of pulling it off, and Linda didn't need to weigh in any further. The rest of the committee quickly understood the realities of budget and time (it was a common topic at the marketing committee meeting). They spent a little while discussing whether there was a cheaper way to film this, until another board member had an idea: they didn't have to film it at all! The Historical Society could send the costumed volunteers to the popular Smallville farmers market and get the same result! Instead of one or two people in a shop seeing the costumed volunteers, a whole bunch of people at the market would. The volunteers could talk in character to the farmers about planting crops, they could pretend to be amazed by the food trucks at the market, they could talk to parents they met about child-rearing in the 1850s. Best of all—it was *free*. All the worries about equipment and cost went away.

Everyone, including both Dennis and Linda, got really excited by the idea. They started making plans for how and when to stage their idea.

At the next board meeting, the marketing committee chair (note: not Dennis) presented the new plan, and everyone loved it. One board member said that she had a friend at a local TV station and that she could give her a heads-up about it.

In the end, the market day went great, the costumed volunteers were a big hit with the market-goers, and the historical society even managed to get 30 seconds of coverage about the costumed volunteers at the end of the local news broadcast.

Just as importantly, the board saved a lot of time and headaches. Dennis's idea was appropriately channeled into something usable. The marketing committee showed their worth. A group is often smarter than any single person, and that definitely held true for them: no individual person—including Dennis and Linda—would have come up with this plan on their own. They all needed to be in the room together thinking about it constructively.

And, finally, the relationships between board members and between board and staff were still strong (and actually strengthened).

––––––––

Here's an important note to this whole scenario. Even if the marketing committee hadn't found a way to make the idea happen, this process still would have been better than the alternative for the time saved and preservation of the emotional energy of everyone involved. The marketing committee as a whole—*not just Linda*—would have collectively decided that Dennis's idea wouldn't work within the constraints of their budget and time. Maybe they would have identified a means of applying for a grant for a video camera, or maybe not. Maybe they would have suggested finding room in next year's budget to hire a company, or maybe not. But that result would be coming after a robust conversation between board members—board members *equal* to Dennis, and not his supposed "employee." Dennis would have felt his idea had been given a fair hearing, so even a negative decision—while disappointing—would be understandable, and likely wouldn't cause rifts later.

It's the supervisor/employee relationship that can make the tendency of a board member to casually throw out ideas to the executive director so problematic, which is why this section on using the committee structure of the board comes here. Participating in a robust committee structure is the way to be most helpful to your board. Working outside of it will make a lot more work for the executive director and your fellow board members who have to try to rein you back in.

## A board has one employee

There's another important point to make here when it comes to how a board member interacts with the executive director: she is the *only* employee the board has. Everyone else works for her.

Imagine a nonprofit as a sort of hourglass. At the top of the hourglass is the board. The narrow pinch in the middle is the executive director. And below her at the base of the hourglass are staff and volunteers. Those staff and volunteers report to her, and to her alone.

In the same way that board members should not individually assign tasks to an executive director, they should not do the same to staff beneath her. The executive director manages their time, their priorities, and their workload—not the board. So it's hard on employees to know what to do when a board member calls them and asks them to do something if they already have a full plate.

I'll repeat: requests and ideas should go through board committees, and those committees can decide whether to ask for more information or support from an executive director. It's then her decision on how to handle it. Can she delegate it? Can she do it herself? She knows the capabilities and workloads of the staff and volunteers better than anyone. It's her call to make.

### A quick note on "firing" an executive director

I've devoted a longer section to the question of terminating the employment of an executive director in the "How to Be Board President" chapter in the back. It's there because this is a responsibility for the board president to manage and lead.

As a new board member you should know a few things about this sensitive topic. I hope you don't have to go through the process, but if you do, here are a few things to keep in mind.

First, if a board member sidles up to you in the parking lot after a meeting and drops hints about possibly firing the executive director or "going in a new direction" with the position, that board member is seriously speaking out of turn. This topic is a big deal. Don't engage in gossip about it. *If there are truly issues that warrant consideration of letting the executive director go, you should talk about it in only two places: one-on-one with the board president, or in executive session as a full board.* That's how you know it's serious.

Second, if there really are issues with the executive director's performance and the topic of firing an executive director is actually on the table, you might feel pressure from other board members or your board president to decide unanimously to release the person. Your duty as a board member is to vote in the manner that *you* feel is best. If you don't think someone deserves to be fired, vote that way, no matter the social pressure.

(The same holds true for hiring an executive director. If you don't think someone should be hired, don't vote for the person. Yes, there will be a record of your dissenting vote and you will have to own your vote to the new executive director if he or she is hired. But you should vote the way you feel is right.)

Third, you should personally become familiar with the employment contract of your executive director, if there is one. Your board may choose to get a lawyer to protect itself during this process, but you should spend the time educating yourself as well.

Fourth, once the decision has been voted on and approved by the board—even if you voted against it—now your job *is* to be a team player. Even if you cast a dissenting vote, you have an obligation to support the nonprofit and to not undermine the board because you disagreed with them. That means you should not warn the director that it's coming. You should not call her up immediately afterward and commiserate about how unfair it was. If there is media interest in the story (and there often can be, because a nonprofit usually distributes a press release after it has fired an executive director), you should not answer media inquires but instead refer all comments to the board president or the designated spokesperson. Often there is a non-disclosure agreement signed between the board and the departing executive director to protect the reputation of both parties. In that case, you *really* don't want to be the one to break it.

## Back to Dennis

"So it seems like when it comes to supervising Linda, there isn't actually a lot that I personally should be doing," Dennis said.

"In most normal times, not really," the board president agreed. "I ask for feedback twice a year on performance and when I hear the same comment from a few board members, I pass that on to Linda so she can improve. If something were going really wrong, or if Linda took a new job and we had to hire a new executive director then there would be more to do. But we're not like a traditional boss watching to see what time she punches the clock. We *can't* be—we're simply not there. How she communicates with us, how she fixes problems or mistakes, and how the overall nonprofit is doing are the best ways we can see how she is furthering the mission."

## A board manages itself

"The truth is," the board president continued, "just keeping ourselves on track is hard enough without worrying about what Linda's doing every second of every day. That's because the final big responsibility we have as a board is to manage ourselves."

"That sounds like something that comes with being in your seat," Dennis said.

The board president laughed. "Maybe it looks that way. I just try to keep everyone going in roughly the same direction. But it only works if other board members step up. The governance committee needs to meet regularly and set an action plan for the year. I can't be too involved in that; there's just no time. And if a meeting is in danger of going long, the board needs more people to be conscious of the clock than just me. Making strategic planning a priority on the agenda is always hard. We all have to be invested in it, or it's just a pet project of mine and it will be abandoned as soon as I step down."

Notice that the board president is talking about two different ways that the board manages itself: through formal and informal means.

Formally, a board should have policies about how it operates. Are there term limits on board members? Is there a governance committee that reviews how the board does its business and makes recommendations? Is there a conflict-of-interest policy that board members are asked to sign? Who makes sure they do so? These are formal roles of how a board manages itself.

There are also informal ways that a board manages itself. These are often called "norms" or a "board culture." Are there expectations that the meeting will start on time? How does a board deal with conflict during a board meeting? Are there "parking lot" meetings after the board meeting where the real business happens? Are quiet people encouraged to speak up? Do individual board members feel empowered or does all the work reside with the board president? If a committee is falling apart, who helps put the pieces back together?

Cultural norms are powerful and self-reinforcing, and their effect on how the board conducts its business can be strong. Pay attention to them and look for opportunities to make changes if there are norms you'd like to improve.

The formal and informal ways that a board manages itself are a clear responsibility of the board. No one else can do it for you. (I speak from early experience on that point: an executive director who tries to weigh in on how the board handles its business will meet with a distinctly icy response.)

## Individual responsibilities

"And so that's about the whole of it," the board president concluded his (rather long) answer to Dennis. "We ensure we're following the mission, create policy, ensure the financial health of the Historical Society, help with fundraising, work on the strategic plan, supervise Linda, and handle the board's governance."

Dennis nodded. "That makes it more clear what the board itself does. I hadn't ever really thought about it before. But I'm still trying to figure out if this is a good fit for me. I guess I still need to get a better handle on what's expected of me personally, and what I could bring."

The board president had gone over the expected time of his meeting with Dennis, but he was glad to do so. He appreciated how much thought Dennis was giving to the idea, and that he hadn't just agreed on the spot.

"Some of those questions like 'Is this a good fit for me'—only you can answer for yourself," he said. "But I can cover what we expect of our board members.

"In addition to some of the duties we've talked about, such as fundraising, we have a few other expectations. For example, we ask that you do your best to attend all board meetings and that you sit on one board committee. We have what we call a 'memorandum of understanding' that spells it all out. We ask new members to sign it when they join, and everyone signs it at the first meeting of the fiscal year. Here's a copy you can take home with you and think about."

A memorandum of understanding

An "MOU" is a good way for a board to make sure it is clear with its members about what's expected of them. If the board that you are joining doesn't have anything this formal, the responsibilities listed below probably get to some of the "unstated" expectations that a board has for its members.

(Along with other useful documents, there is a full copy of a sample memorandum of understanding available in a special download section at http://forsmallnonprofits.com/boarddocs.)

Here are some responsibilities that a board might ask an individual member to agree to:

- I will communicate the organization's work and values to the community and represent the organization when requested.
- I will attend at least 80 percent of board meetings.
- I will be a member of at least one committee and attend at least 80 percent of its meetings.
- I will make my best effort to attend special events.
- I will give a financial contribution to the Annual Fund, making the organization a priority in my philanthropy.
- I will actively participate in one or more fundraising activity.
- I will act in the best interests of the organization and excuse myself from discussions and votes where I have a conflict of interest.
- I will stay informed about what's going on in the organization. I will ask questions and request information. I will participate in and take responsibility for making decisions on issues, policies, and other board matters.

- I will work in good faith with staff and other board members as partners toward achievement of our goals.
- I will regularly review the financial position of the nonprofit and remain engaged when it is time to annually adopt a budget.
- If I don't fulfill these commitments to the organization, I will expect the board president or president-elect to call me and discuss my responsibilities with me.

### More than just responsibilities

Dennis knew now that he wanted to join the board. The responsibilities of the board and the expectations they had for him seemed reasonable. But there were still some key questions he had for the board president that would help him determine whether the board was a good fit.

### When are the meetings?

"Meetings are the third Tuesday night of the month, 5:00 to 6:30, although we have been known to run a few minutes long," the board president replied.

This is a basic question of whether you can join a board. If the regular monthly meetings are a direct conflict for you, you can't join the board in good faith, no matter how much you want to.

How long is a board member's term? Are there term limits?

"The Historical Society has three-year terms for all our board members, renewable once. So you could step down after three years, or choose to stay and serve a full six years."

Many boards have standard terms, often between two and four years, that are renewable once or twice. This protects the nonprofit from having a board stagnate, but also gives the volunteer board member a clear expectation of their window of service. In other words, it gives them an out. Six or eight years on a board can burn out a volunteer. Terms and term limits let them exit gracefully. Many boards don't have term limits, which is not the worst thing in the world. But a board that doesn't have any terms at all suggests the board has not given much thought to its governance structure.

How I am elected?

"A majority vote of the board is required to put you on the slate of candidates, and then at our annual meeting with the full membership, we present the slate for a voice vote by the membership. It's a formality at this point, but we didn't want a possible fight with the membership about getting rid of their vote and appointing board members ourselves."

Many boards elect new members at the last meeting of the fiscal year, and then the new members attend the next meeting. There's nothing unusual there. You're elected, and you're on.

Sometimes, though, board members are elected only at a special annual meeting of the full membership of the organization (as distinct from board members). Knowing whether you will need to be elected by the membership is useful. Knowing if this election is competitive is even more important. It's good to know if you run the risk of standing for nomination to the board and losing to someone else. Maybe you'll want to run anyway, but this should not be a surprise. Ask.

## Do you have D&O insurance?

"Of course."

Most nonprofits, even small ones, carry directors and officers liability insurance on behalf of their board.

D&O insurance protects the board members from liability that might arise from doing their duty as a board member. If someone sues the nonprofit, and the nonprofit loses, instead of each board member having to pay their equal share, the insurance company steps in. The main exception, usually, is negligence.

Very small nonprofits, though, may not carry this insurance so it's worth asking about.

## What documents can you give me to review before I decide?

"I'll email you the draft of the strategic plan we're working on, the MOU, the current budget, and the last two board packets for your review."

It's good to get your hands on whatever documents you can. Ask for the current budget, the most recent financial report given to board members, the bylaws, a strategic plan (if it exists), and the minutes and agendas from the last meeting or two. You'll get a good sense from those documents of the business of the board and the nonprofit.

From those documents, here are some things to look for:

- *How much money is in the bank?* (This is on the balance sheet.) You can compare this to the monthly expenditures on the profit and loss statement and get a rough idea of how many "months of reserves" the nonprofit has. For example, a nonprofit with $20,000 in the bank and regular monthly expenses of $7,000 has slightly less than three months of reserves. This is a useful number to know, since it will give you a sense of how much time a nonprofit has to adapt to changing revenue or other surprises. At least three months of reserves is a good number to see. Less than a month should merit more questions. (There might be a good explanation.)

- *Is there a strategic plan?* Does it make sense to you? Many very small nonprofits might not have a strategic plan in writing, and that's probably nothing to worry about. But the larger the nonprofit, the more you should expect to see one.
- *Do the minutes and the agenda show that the board is doing work you are interested in doing and that a board should be doing?* If the minutes show that the board spent a lot of time discussing and approving the design of the most recent marketing booklet— something that is clearly not one of the primary tasks of a board, and likely shouldn't even make it onto its agenda—then you may want to give a second thought to joining. It's possible that the board doesn't know what its primary tasks are. Again, ask for more information.

## Do you like going to board meetings?

This question caused the board president to stop short. He hadn't expected anything like that. Sometimes the meetings were a little boring, and sometimes they were a little tense. But generally, he realized, yes. He really did look forward to doing the work of the board.

Except in dire circumstances, being on a board should be enjoyable. There is a real camaraderie that can develop among board members. You have a common interest, and together you are forging a common vision for the nonprofit's future. That will help you form new relationships that might last well beyond your term on the board.

If the work is good, and the people are good, being on a board can be a rewarding experience. I sincerely hope that the questions in this chapter will help you determine whether a particular board is the right place for you to experience that.

Dennis had heard enough and read enough about the Smallville Historical Society board to believe he was ready to join a board for the first time.

TWO

# YOUR FIRST JOB: ATTENDING MEETINGS

IN TERMS of actual time logged, your experience on a board will be mostly spent either in meetings or reading documents in preparation for meetings.

Learning how these meetings work and being ready to participate will help you be as good a board member as you can be. But again—you have to show up.

## Preparing for a board meeting

*Know when the meeting is well in advance.*

You should add all of the meetings to your calendar as soon as you know the dates and times. Hopefully your board has a set time and place for the meeting that doesn't change often. If so, you should schedule them out for the whole year. It's understandable if a family vacation causes you to miss a board meeting. But if you wind up missing a board meeting because you scheduled something that just as easily could have been any other day, you'll find that you miss too many meetings to really know what's going on or to contribute meaningfully. Plan it out!

. . .

*Read all the material.*

You should receive a "board packet" via email from the executive director or board president that has all of the information you will need for the meeting. This often includes the agenda, the minutes from the last meeting, the monthly financial report, some written committee reports, and maybe draft policies or other action items.

I recommend at least glancing at the agenda as soon as it arrives to see if there's something on it to which you might be expected to contribute. Try to read the financials and the written reports at least a day before the meeting. Go ahead and email your board president or a relevant committee chair with clarifying questions before the meeting if you feel that you need help understanding the documents. (New board members often feel that they are on a steep learning curve. As a frequent board member and an executive director, I can say that you should totally feel comfortable asking for help before, during, or after meetings.)

*Eat. Use the bathroom.*

Some of us turn into bears if we haven't eaten in a while. Don't go to a board meeting on an empty stomach. Eat something. Empty your bladder. Drink coffee if you need it. A board meeting that might already be a little dry or a little long will get even more so if you're hungry or have to go to the bathroom.

*Show up five minutes early.*

Plan to arrive five minutes early to make sure you aren't in a rush and have time to chat with your fellow board members socially. If you don't know exactly where the meeting room is, though, or aren't sure where to find parking, then budget an extra five minutes to give yourself time to figure it out.

You should be ready when the meeting starts.

*Dress up... a bit.*

Board meetings for most small nonprofits are not formal affairs. You don't need to don a suit and tie or business blazer. But I wouldn't recommend showing up in flip-flops and a tank top either. You might not be getting paid, but it's still work.

Here on the West Coast, I would suggest aiming for "business casual" (we rarely dress up more than that anyway), but your community or region might have a different standard of dress for work. What level of dress do you see the employees of the nonprofit wearing? They are working for the nonprofit just like you are. They can be a good model for the meeting. Again— if you are really not sure, ask the board president.

### At the meeting

Dennis was ready for his first board meeting. He'd read the material, he'd planned extra time to find parking, and he'd had a big snack. He was ready to go. This was the agenda in front of him.

5:00 - Call to order
Welcome guests
Approve consent agenda
5:05 - Introduction of a historical artifact
5:10 - President's report
5:15 - Executive director's report
5:20 - Treasurer's report

5:35 - Governance committee report – new policy proposal
5:45 - Strategic planning
6:20 - Board comments
6:25 - Executive session
6:30 - Adjourn


(I want to point out that the structure above is a good summation of what I think an *ideal* board meeting looks like. It's short—about 90 minutes long. The first half is for the easy stuff. The second half is reserved for one big thing each meeting: the budget, the bylaws, strategic planning, a second or a third strategic planning session, fundraising, and other big topics that deserve the time. I think it's a great model. There's also a sample agenda in Word doc form available at http:// forsmallnonprofits.com/boarddocs.)

I'm going to go through this meeting in close detail for two main reasons. The first is that new board members should get an idea of what the flow of a board meeting might be like. The second is that the structure of the meeting above is one that more nonprofits should choose to emulate. So, as you read through it, you might see some ways that your board meeting could shave some minutes off the clock or handle issues differently.

Let's go through this agenda line by line.


*5:00 - Call to order*

The call to order at many board meetings often doesn't happen at 5:00 (or whenever the prescribed start time is). The board president allows a couple minutes for stragglers, and suddenly the meeting starts at 5:05 or 5:10 instead of 5:00. Not good!

Fortunately the board president of the Historical Society is a stickler. He wants to get people out on time, and that means starting on time. When he became president he gave everyone a fair warning that meetings would start on time. It took only a few meetings when members arrived late to realize he was serious.

*Welcome guests*

Generally speaking, board meetings are open to the public, or at least to your organization's membership, if that applies. What happens at board meetings is not a secret. This agenda item is a good reminder that the public is welcome, and should be welcomed at the beginning of the meeting by the president.

You might be a newbie at the first meeting and feel like a guest yourself. That's OK. Soon you'll be on the "inside" and you can welcome guests before a meeting with a smile and a handshake.

*The consent agenda: approving noncontroversial items together*

Approving the agenda and the minutes separately takes up valuable time—especially considering that there are usually no changes or corrections. Boards have started to address this by creating something called the "consent agenda." A consent agenda bundles all sorts of noncontroversial items into a single item on the agenda that is passed without discussion.

The most common items are the meeting agenda and previous meeting's minutes. If your board has to approve other easy tasks—partnerships with another organization, appointing a non-board member to a committee—this could go in the consent agenda, too. Any basic item that the board president thinks doesn't need discussion is a good candidate. The consent agenda should be sent out in advance with the board packet.

At the Smallville Historical Society board meeting, when the board president got to that item on the agenda, he asked if anyone would like to pull an item from the consent agenda for further discussion and a separate vote. Dennis didn't say anything. It all seemed basic enough to him. No one else did either. (That's the great thing about the consent agenda. Most of the time, nothing changes. If someone does ask for something to be considered separately, that item gets placed next on the agenda.)

After a period of a few seconds of silence, the board president said, "I'm looking for a motion to approve the consent agenda."

Someone said, "So moved!"

A moment later, someone else said, "Second!"

"All those in favor?" the board president asked.

Everyone said, "Aye."

"Any opposed?" the board president asked as a formality. "OK. Consent agenda is approved."

It happened in less than ten seconds. Dennis barely even had time to vote "Aye," he was so surprised. That's why consent agendas can be so useful. Normally after a motion is presented there is discussion. A benefit of the consent agenda is that no discussion is needed—that's why board members have a chance to pull something from the agenda for further discussion and why it's the only vote where the question of "any opposed?" truly is just a formality. By structuring the meeting this way, a good deal of needless air is compressed out of a meeting.

(If you have questions about the business of "so moved" and "second," I cover the basics of motions and voting in Appendix A on *Robert's Rules of Order*.)

*5:05 - Introduction of a historical artifact*

Every month, Linda brings an artifact from the pioneer cabin and explains what it is and its historical significance to the board. What is that all about? It seemed out of place to Dennis.

Simply put, it's easy for a board to lose the forest for the trees. So much of a board meeting is about governance and fundraising and budgets that board members can often use a reminder about why they are working so hard. At the Grand Cinema board meetings we often started with a five-minute movie clip. A social services nonprofit could read a statement from a member who's been served. An environmental nonprofit could start every meeting with a reminder of the number of acres of forest it has conserved. An animal shelter could bring a kitten or puppy for the first five minutes. None of these ideas should take a lot of time, although staff will have to prepare something, so if it's too onerous (like bringing a cat), this could happen every other month or quarterly. But it sets an important tone for the rest of the meeting: *We're all working together, and this is why we do it.*

*5:10 - President's report*

The president began his report by recognizing the new members who had joined the board. He asked them to introduce themselves, and then asked everyone else on the board to give their name. After that, he laid out his main priority for the year—that the Historical Society continue its work on the strategic plan and that the board schedule a retreat in a few months.

What else might a president say during his report? Often, it might be nothing more than saying, "We have a lot of work on the budget tonight, so let's keep things moving." The president could report on a recent executive committee meeting, some recent news, or some other strategic goal. Whatever is covered, there should not be an expectation that the president will use the full five minutes.

(The introductions of new board members obviously took more time than a regular president's report, but the Historical Society's board meeting was only a few minutes behind schedule.)

### 5:15 - *Executive director's report*

Once the president's report was concluded, Linda gave her report. Dennis had read her written report already, which was part of the board packet, and noticed that she only touched on a few of the highlights from the written report and updated the board on anything that had changed in the week since it had gone out.

There were a fair number of questions, and a few questions made it clear to Dennis that those board members hadn't read Linda's report in advance. He felt a little better for having been prepared.

Eventually, the president said they had time for one more question before moving along to the next item. Linda said she was happy to answer any further questions by phone.

They were now about five minutes late in their agenda.

### 5:20 - *Treasurer's report*

The financial information had been sent in advance with the board packet, and Dennis felt on much less certain ground. He thought he got the gist of it, but he wasn't sure. The report had come with a "dashboard" of helpful numbers and graphs that were intended to show the financial picture of the organization at a glance. In addition, the packet also contained a profit and loss statement for the month, with a comparison to budget;

a year-to-date profit and loss statement for the fiscal year, with a comparison to budget; and a balance sheet. Thanks to an earlier orientation, he was pretty clear on what the dashboard was telling him and what the profit and loss statement meant (it showed a profit, which seemed good). But the balance sheet really threw him. They'd explained it at orientation several times and finally he just said he understood it, even though he still wasn't sure.

At the meeting, the treasurer began reviewing the key information on the dashboard and gave it a quick gloss-over. He was acting as a sort of interpreter for the numbers, highlighting the ones he and the finance committee felt were important.

"You'll see in the first graph on page one that ..."

"Going to page two, the important take-away here is that while revenue was down, we still managed to stay..."

"Membership is down year to date, but we believe there have been seasonal changes. This will be the number to watch next month when we expect to know whether this has corrected itself."

After having gone through the report, the treasurer invited Linda to add a comment. She added only, "You'll see our giving is well over budget this month, thanks to the great annual giving drive led by the board."

Then the treasurer asked for any questions. There were a few questions about specific programs and line items, until finally Dennis got up the courage to ask his own question. "I know this might be familiar to everyone else, but I'm still having trouble with the balance sheet. For example, why is there $1,200 listed as a liability for prepaid sponsorships. Do we owe sponsorship dollars to someone?"

The treasurer nodded and explained that their nonprofit used a style of accounting called "accrual" and then explained how it affected the balance sheet.

Dennis thought he understood it, but he still wasn't sure.

"If it's helpful, why don't you and I meet and look at a series of last year's balance sheets and profit and loss statements," the treasurer suggested. "I will show you how the money moved between the two."

"That would be really great, thank you."

The board member next to Dennis suddenly perked up, "Actually, can I come to that meeting as well? Your description made me realize I don't really understand how that works."

The treasurer said he would send an invitation to the whole board, and then they were ready to move on. Dennis had been worried about exposing the fact that he didn't understand the balance sheet, but he felt that he'd gotten a slightly better handle on it (and discovering he wasn't the only one who didn't get it made him feel better, too).

———

At this point, after the treasurer's report has been submitted, some boards formally vote to "accept" the report. There is actually no reason for this convention. What would it mean if you voted no? That you didn't "accept" it for some reason? The best reason I can think of to vote to accept the treasurer's report is that it reaffirms the board's fiscal oversight duty. But even then, the board has a lot of other duties that don't get this treatment. The treasurer's report doesn't need to be special.

If you're working to shave time from your meeting, I'd remove this. Being at the board meeting, hearing the financial report, and asking appropriate questions is how a board does its due diligence. You don't need a special motion to approve the report.

.  .  .

*5:35 - Governance committee report – new policy proposal*

After the treasurer's report, the Smallville Historical Society moved on to the governance committee report. The chair of the committee distributed a first draft of a proposal for a "conflict of interest statement" that asked board members to disclose any partner organizations or individuals they had a financial relationship with and to agree to recuse themselves if needed ("recuse" means to abstain from both commenting and voting). The draft had been included in the packet. There were a few questions about what "counted" and what didn't, and the committee chair answered all of those. There were a few questions about wording and the chair agreed that the committee would look at it during its next meeting.

"We could probably fix it right here, but since we generally don't like to ask for a vote on a new policy the first time we see it, we can just bring the revisions forward at the next meeting when we vote on this," the governance chair said.

Ten minutes had been budgeted, but the committee used only five. Suddenly the meeting was back on time again.

Notice that none of the other committees were listed on the agenda. The only time a committee should be on the agenda is when it wants to bring a particular item forward for discussion (in preparation for a vote), or when it wants to bring an item forward for a vote. If a committee doesn't have a specific piece of business for a vote or discussion, but still wants to update the board, it should submit a written report in the board packet.

*5:45 - Strategic planning*

The board president summed up for the new board members strategic planning work done to date, and reiterated his belief that the Smallville Historical Society was at a turning point for the organization. The board wanted to stay on top of strategic planning by giving it priority at meetings when needed. It wouldn't be at every meeting, the president noted, but the board had the space for it when needed because it had streamlined its entire agenda to allow time for one big topic. Some nights the second half of the meeting would be used to talk about the budget, or fundraising, but tonight the focus was on strategic planning.

With 35 minutes scheduled for strategic planning—more than twice the time allotted to anything else on the agenda—the board can actually get a lot done. Can the board create a whole strategic plan in that amount of time? No. But it can brainstorm, think big, or listen to a presentation from a consultant or board member who is tasked with leading the planning. Over the course of several meetings with this on the agenda, a board will have put in a lot of work on an important subject.

6:20 - *Board comments*

The board president wrapped up the strategic planning portion of the meeting and asked if there were any board comments. One board member thanked the new members for joining the board. Another commented that the state history museum had a great photo exhibit that included some photos of Smallville. Another passed on a conversation he'd had with a donor about the donor's frustration trying to register for an event online instead of by phone as he was used to.

The board president jumped in and reminded everyone that Linda had made the strategic decision to use an online ticketing service to handle events to save time and money, and that event registration seemed to be increasing because of it. Linda promised she would call the donor to see if she could help him out.

(A lot of negative comments in this unstructured time can

be difficult to manage. It's not a gripe session. Additionally, it's a good idea not to act on everything that is raised. All too often, people just want to get out of the meeting and they'll nod their heads at anything someone says. Don't assign tasks during this time because someone has a complaint. If something really does need to be dealt with, it can be sent to a committee for further work and decision-making.)

6:25 - *Executive session*

The board president reserved five minutes for an executive session at the end of the meeting to talk about a personnel issue. Executive sessions limit the number of people in the room—usually all guests are asked to step out, and sometimes the executive director. No minutes are taken during executive session and no votes take place. The most frequent reasons for an executive session involve personnel, legal issues or litigation, and real estate or other contractual negotiations that a board doesn't want to be leaked.

Once Linda had left, the board president started the executive session by saying, "Last month, two board members told me that they received angry calls from a normally generous donor to the Historical Society who was personally upset with Linda, and was withholding his donation because of it. I had coffee with the donor to discuss his concerns. He is upset that Linda and our curator are not willing to put his family's historical photographs on display in the cabin.

"I spoke to Linda to find out her side of the story—she did admit that she had probably been too dismissive of his requests and she apologized to me for that and said she would apologize to him.

"That said, from what I can tell, Linda and the curator are in the right—the photos were almost certainly taken many decades after the founding of Smallville and don't fit the focus on the pioneer days that we've all agreed is our priority.

"During my meeting with Linda, she suggested that a couple of his photos of the bell tower under construction were good enough that we could create an exhibit of the bell tower through the decades off-site from the pioneer cabin—maybe even in the lobby of the bell tower. I thought it was a good idea, and it should go a long way toward smoothing things over with our donor.

"I just wanted to bring it to everyone's attention and let you know how Linda will be moving forward. This was brought to me as a possible personnel issue about Linda's behavior, which is why it came up during an executive session, but I think everything's been smoothed over with the donor now that Linda's apologized and we've found this solution. Are there any questions?"

Dennis didn't have any and there were only two or three questions before they went back out of executive session.

*A note on discussing personnel in executive session*

Discussing personnel in an executive session is always preferable to the "parking lot" meetings that might happen, where board members gossip or vent in small cliques after the meeting. If some board members bring forward an issue about the executive director, it is usually appropriate to discuss it with the full board. Even though it lets everyone else in on a "problem" that they didn't know about before, the advantage is that there is not a divide between board members who are "in the know" and those who aren't. (Not every issue necessarily should go to the full board, of course, but for many issues it is the right way to go.)

The president should take care that executive session does

not become a dump session on the executive director just because she's left the room. If one person vents about an issue, the president can choose to take it up with the executive director, or not. If there is serious criticism of the performance of the executive director during this time, then the president or the executive committee may need to take what they're hearing and schedule a separate meeting to discuss it further. They should generally not attempt to solve it there as the full board. As with committees, it can be useful to have a small group take information and feedback at one meeting, and then come back at the next and report its recommendation.

Generally speaking, there should not be any board business following an executive session, unless you've instructed your executive director to wait around to return to the meeting. If you think there will be business after an executive session, you should be clear about that when you ask guests to leave—something like, "We will go into executive session for thirty minutes to discuss a contractual issue." If you need to go longer, just let your guests, or the executive director, know.

*One idea: a standing executive session*

Some boards—and I have worked for one that did this—have a standing executive session on the schedule at the end of the meeting, without staff or guests present.

When an executive session gets added to the schedule at the last minute, sometimes executive directors get nervous. Even if they know the reason for the executive session, they may still worry. So the idea of placing a standing executive session on the agenda means that the executive director doesn't have extra cause to worry because a board member requested an executive session at the last minute.

That said, the executive director probably isn't going to like this idea. I didn't like it much when my board met without me for five minutes at the end of every meeting, although I could see the reasoning behind it. But if it's an idea that could be helpful to you and your board, I wanted to make sure you were aware of it.

### 6:30 - *Adjourn*

This part is easy. The president says, "Unless there is other business, I will entertain a motion to adjourn the meeting." Someone moves to adjourn, someone seconds it, and the president adjourns the meeting.

And look at that! The meeting is done in ninety minutes.

## Decorum and handling dissent at board meetings

A board is at its best when there is debate and discussion about the important matters affecting the nonprofit. If there are differences of opinion, this should be a *real* debate. All points of view should be heard.

How that works in practice, however, is much harder. The first step is making sure you know how to voice your own opinion.

### *On speaking up*

Knowing how to act at board meetings can be tricky for someone who has never been to one before.

Some people get onto a board and are afraid to say anything for fear of saying the wrong thing or exposing their ignorance. *As a rule of thumb, I think it's important to speak up or ask a question at least once every meeting.* You are on a board to have a voice. Use it!

Sometimes just being the person to "sum up" what you've heard so far is important, even if you don't have a strong opinion you want to share. (This kind of active "observing" can be helpful for the other board members to better see where their differences are without the emotion of an argument getting in the way.)

Others feel similarly anxious but express it by talking *too* much. If you find yourself talking a lot during a board meeting and you are not the president of the board, then consider testing yourself to remain silent during a motion or two. Yes, of course, if it seems there will be a split vote or otherwise two different sides, you can jump in. But most votes aren't like that. And in giving yourself the freedom to just sit back and watch every so often, you might learn something about yourself.

*Advocating for a position*

How do you advocate for what you believe without belittling someone else or their ideas? That's a key question for all board members. People come at this from all over the map.

Some people may have a hard time telling someone they "disagree" with them. It's just not in their nature. Others may be used to heated arguments and won't even register that there is real disagreement until someone's voice is raised. Different people approach conflict differently. Your fellow board members will have different ideas about how to conduct themselves during a disagreement or an argument than you do. *Guaranteed.*

One idea that will help you present your ideas more clearly is starting them with the phrase "I feel" or "In my opinion" (so long as the sentence that follows is not "that you're an idiot"). Using this construction, you are more likely to be clear about your idea and you are less likely to target someone else personally. In short, you have a better chance of being understood. I've seen people who are so afraid to state their opinion, that their message is lost in all their conditions and clauses.

Let's consider these three statements and their alternatives:

*"No way! Recent history is boring and no one cares about it. We need to stick to the exciting parts, like the early pioneers."*

This dismisses someone else's feelings as irrelevant.

Alternatively: "I think that we should focus on the pioneer days, which has long been our focus, and not the entirety of Smallville's history."

*"I don't know, Bob... with the way the finances are... and the reserves... what if...? I mean, if in five years something ... you know, changes at the state... Then where would the cabin be?"*

This isn't clear at all. Bob might be able to parse it out, but he's just as likely not to know what you're getting at.

Alternatively: "I have to disagree, Bob. In my opinion, we are running a real financial risk by continuing to rely on the state grant for operation of the cabin."

*"Do you think that if you looked at the committee report from the point of view of finances that you might see why it's obvious to everyone else but you that we need to raise our dues?"*

Again, this belittles the person, but does it through the sneaky way of asking them a question. If you want to ask someone a question, ask them a question. If you want to advocate for an idea, advocate for an idea. Don't mix them up.

Alternatively: "Based on the report from the finance

committee, I feel that we need to seriously look at raising fees to cover expenses."

In addition to your words and your tone, you should be aware of your body language. Are you domineering and physically using your size to try to get your way (unconsciously or not). Are you practically curling up into a ball as you speak? Are you talking to someone while looking at them over your reading glasses? (If there is a significant age gap, this will come off to the younger person as condescending.)

All in all, be polite but clear. Remember that everyone in the room is there because they support the work of the nonprofit. Even if they disagree with you on the means to do so. The tone of a board meeting and the board as a whole is formed over time. There is more detail about managing dissent and discussion in the chapter on being board president.

*Listening during board meetings*

Just as important as advocating for your position is listening to others and what they believe is best for the nonprofit. A board with a variety of experiences and viewpoints produces the best results, but that works only if board members are willing to listen to one another.

Why is someone advocating for a position that you disagree with? What do they see that you don't? It's important that you attempt to understand where someone is coming from. Give them the benefit of the doubt and think about their argument. Sometimes you might see a new side of a discussion you hadn't considered before. Sometimes you won't, but it's good to know where your fellow board member is coming from.

Try to phrase back to them what you're hearing, without

overloaded judgment. "What I'm hearing from you, Barb, is that you are worried that term limits will hurt our board, because new board members might not replace the good quality board members that we already have. Is that correct?"

Barb, in that example, should be willing to confirm it or clarify. But it's not a window for her to start talking again. Once you've confirmed it, you should get your chance to reply with your opinion.

*In the end, vote and move on.*

It's entirely possible you won't get to consensus on every issue, no matter how much you listen to one another. That's totally fine. At some point, the board will need to vote. It may be a split vote, and while that may not happen often, it's important not to hold grudges whether you are on the winning side of the vote or the losing side.

Done right, a board's camaraderie and shared sense of purpose should be strong enough to get through split votes without lingering resentment.

## After the meeting

*Avoid "parking lot" meetings.*

Sometimes boards can fall into the habit of having "parking lot" meetings where the "real work" is done. That's where they share their real feelings about a controversial new policy proposed by a governance committee—and not in the meeting in front of everyone.

Parking lot meetings can sometimes happen with good intentions ("Hey, Fred, do you have a second to explain accrual accounting now?"). Or maybe someone didn't think of an issue until afterwards (this is why it's a good idea for a board not to pass a new policy at the same meeting where it first sees it).

Parking lot meetings get problematic when someone uses them to steer the course of a board without having to advocate openly for an idea in the meeting ("Hey, Barb, I thought that there were some real problems with that new proposal, didn't you?")

Again, if there are real problems, those should come up in the meeting, or should be saved until feedback can be given at a committee meeting or the next board meeting.

Some board members may try to build a coalition of support for their ideas between meetings with one-on-one phone calls or meetings, as if they are counting votes. Your board shouldn't have the same amount of political jockeying as Congress. Yes, feel free to check in with a trusted board member on an idea before you present it. Hear what the person has to say. But the work of the board should take place in committees and board meetings, not gathered in a clique of three or four people around a car door.

I urge you, as a new board member, not to participate. You may gain the short-term satisfaction of feeling that you're running with the in-crowd, but it will be at the expense of the long-term benefit of improving the board's communications and professionalism.

*Self-evaluation*

I have seen boards use surveymonkey.com or other online (and anonymous) polls to solicit feedback about how a board meeting went. Such a survey contains a one-through-five rating scale and asks three or four questions (but no more than that!). Some ideas for questions could be:

- Overall, how was the board meeting?
- Did the board spend its time during the meeting on its principal duties and responsibilities (as you understand them)?
- Did the board listen to all voices who wanted to speak?
- Do you have additional comments about how the board is doing or how the meeting went?

These four questions, answered anonymously, would give a board a very good sense of how it is doing as a group during board meetings. A governance chair, board secretary, or the executive director could create the free surveymonkey.com account and ask these questions. You might consider asking them at every meeting for a few months and then only every so often once the returns become consistent (and consistently positive). Or, if someone is up to the task of collecting and reviewing the information, go ahead and send it every month.

These should be sent within a day or two of a meeting, while information and tone are still fresh in people's minds.

*Think about committee assignments.*

Assignments or tasks referred to committee should be dealt with at the next committee meeting. If you are in a board meeting and you take note of a task given to your committee, jot the note down so that at the meeting you are prepared to take it up. Usually chairs of committees should track these things, but if they don't catch it, you should bring it up so that your committee is prepared to report back at the next meeting.

*Attend committee meetings.*

All board members should serve on a standing committee of the board. "Standing" committees refer to committees that have enough work that they need a regular meeting time. They "stand" on the calendar and members know there will always be work for them.

That time and place should be set at the first meeting of the fiscal year when all members, including new members, are present. (Often these committees will have a time and place that will last for years, longer than any single serving committee member. If it works, it works. Don't mess with it.)

I recommend having at least two standing committees: finance and governance. Even a very small board should be able to fill those two (with the expectation that all board members serve on a committee in addition to being on the board. The only exception is the board president, who often is considered to sit on all of them).

Organizations may also want to consider having a fundraising committee, a marketing committee, a program committee, or a membership committee as standing committees if these are important to the organization. (Technically speaking, marketing and program work should fall under operations and be a responsibility of the executive director. But in my experience, board members often want to venture into operations in some way. Having a committee that can channel ideas from board members can be manageable—though not ideal—for both the board and the executive director. A marketing or program committee commonly serves this function.)

———

A board meeting is an important piece of fulfilling your responsibilities as a board member. For many, the culture and structure of a board meeting can be hard to decipher at first. I hope that by looking at a single board meeting closely, you better understand how meetings work and how to manage conflict or disagreement that occurs within them. Your board meeting may be different, but when you compare it against this board meeting outlined here, hopefully you will have better tools to understand what's happening than if you had gone in blind.

Now that we've covered board meetings in depth, there is plenty to know about being a board member *outside* the meetings. We'll focus on a board member's responsibilities in the next chapter.

# THREE

# BEYOND MEETINGS

MEETINGS MIGHT BE where a lot of the work happens, but there are key responsibilities of a board member outside of meetings. Using the Memorandum of Understanding that Dennis signed when he joined the board as a model, we'll cover some of the common responsibilities and expectations of board members outside of board meetings.

### Common Board Responsibilities

*I will communicate the organization's work and values to the community, and represent the organization when requested.*

This responsibility means that you should be an ambassador of the organization to your friends, colleagues, and families. It also means that you should not be speaking out of turn about budget fights or other intraboard squabbling (should it exist). Be positive and look for opportunities to bring more people into the circle of the nonprofit.

Notice, though, that at the end of this sentence in the MOU there's a bit of a pullback. "When requested" means, for example, that if a reporter calls you to ask questions about a recent issue at the nonprofit, you direct them to the appropriate spokesperson. Knowing when to stay quiet and let the board president or someone else do the talking is just as important as knowing when to boast about the nonprofit's good work to your friends.

*I will make my best effort to attend special events.*

A board member should expect to attend most special events. Visiting with donors, helping behind a registration desk, or just filling out a room so it doesn't feel empty are all helpful ways a board member can contribute. As an executive director, I liked it when board members showed up a few minutes early. There is often a last task that can be done—and if there isn't, the board member is ready to greet other guests as they arrive.

*I will give a financial contribution to the Annual Fund, making the organization a priority in my philanthropy.*

I said earlier that a board member should put the nonprofit ahead of others in giving. My rule of thumb is that if you're on a board, it should be among the top three nonprofits you support financially. Another way to put it is that your gift should be "significant" to you, whatever that means. For a variety of reasons, your board should have 100 percent participation in giving from all board members. Don't be coy and don't make the board president hound you. Give early and give often.

*I will actively participate in one or more fundraising activities.*

As a board member you might be called upon to help with fundraising in a variety of ways. I prefer high-yield activities, but if your board sells raffle tickets (not always a great use of time, but we'll let that go for now), then you should help sell raffle tickets. I like asking board members to call donors to thank them for their gift. A phon-a-thon of board members calling members or donors to ask for gifts can be effective (although fewer and fewer people are picking up their phones these days). Even if there's an hour or two set aside for stuffing envelopes, board members should be willing to help. And you should be expected to fill a table for an annual fundraising event. Don't feel that you have to participate in all activities, but do your best to help when you can.

If you are called upon to do more, such as to actually ask a friend for a donation or a major gift, ask for training and go through some practice runs with your board president or executive director. It's important to get it right.

*I will act in the best interests of the organization and excuse myself from discussions and votes where I have a conflict of interest.*

You need to be on your best behavior about this. If you or a direct family member (usually meaning spouse, child, sibling, or parent) may have a direct financial benefit or loss from a possible vote on the board, you should withdraw from voting and discussion about that issue. If it's a big vote, you should voluntarily leave the room, so that people are willing to be honest without fear of upsetting you.

If you are on a board of another nonprofit organization, you may need to recuse yourself from voting as well. This doesn't occur to as many people because they don't stand to personally gain or lose money either way. But if you have financial responsibilities at two nonprofits, then voting on a contract or partnership may be a conflict of interest.

(An example might be if you are on the board of a nonprofit that is considering a new venue for your regular meetings. The board considers several bids, including the event room at a museum where you are also a board member. The museum will benefit if it gets the contract. In that situation, you should disclose your affiliation to your fellow board members, decline to participate in discussion about the decision, and abstain during voting.)

*I will stay informed about what's going on in the organization. I will ask questions and request information. I will participate in and take responsibility for making decisions on issues, policies, and other board matters.*

Read your emails. Read the organization newsletter. Read the board packet. Read the agenda. And ask for help when you need it.

*I will work in good faith with staff and other board members as partners toward achievement of our goals.*

Working in good faith means that you aren't working at cross purposes with board and staff. You're not trying to get the executive director fired, you're not talking bad about the board president behind his back. It means you're a good team player— a good leader *and* a good follower. Assume the best of people. They are giving their time freely just as you are.

*I will regularly review the financial position of the nonprofit and remain engaged when it is time to annually adopt a budget.*

As discussed several times, this is such a key responsibility that it's beyond just asking questions at meetings. You owe it to the board and the nonprofit to inform yourself on the finances. If you don't understand the numbers presented, sit down one-on-one with the treasurer or attend finance committees and listen in. You won't get it all right away, but do your best to make it a short learning curve.

*If I don't fulfill these commitments to the organization, I will expect the board president or president-elect to call me and discuss my responsibilities with me.*

If you get a hand-slap from your board president, don't take it personally. The board president is trying to wrangle the board members into a cohesive unit. It's a really hard job. If you're making it harder by breaking or bending "the rules" (intentionally or accidentally) then apologize, thank the board president for the reminder of your duties, and do better in the future.

———

While there may be some specific duties a board asks of you that fall outside this list, doing the things listed above will make you a model board member. You'll know you are bringing your best to the organization.

FOUR

# IMPROVING YOUR BOARD

AFTER ATTENDING your first few board meetings, you might discover that the board is not operating at the level you thought it was. Maybe meetings have been surprisingly contentious, with people in heated arguments. Maybe you struggled to stay awake as someone droned on and on at you for two hours. Maybe a board of fifteen people spent forty minutes of the meeting wordsmithing text on the invitation to the fundraiser.

You will need to decide whether you want to stand up and make a suggestion or just roll with it. I recommend making your voice heard. What follows are some ideas that might help you, as the rookie on the board, get change enacted.

Some of these ideas or small fixes might be immediately useful to you. (In my head, I imagine you taking your idea back to your board, and everyone loving it and approving it unanimously.) Some ideas in here will take time, though. An idea that strikes you as exactly what your board needs might be dead on arrival with other members.

This is especially true of a policy that is "good governance" or "best practices." Just because it's "right" doesn't mean that it will fly with your board's norms and cultures. Sometimes these ideas are called "best practices" because they stop certain behaviors—behaviors some of your members would like to continue! So bringing up a new idea might cause some people to feel that you are targeting them (such as discussing term limits when you have some board members who have served a dozen years already).

Keep in mind that not having a policy proposal pass immediately, or in its unvarnished "best practice" form, is OK. (It's the norm, probably.) Don't evaluate success by where you still have to go, but by the progress you've made.

### Join the governance committee

The place to start improving your board is on the governance committee. (Sometimes a board has a "board development" committee, which can take on these kinds of tasks as part of its duties.) This is the place from which new reforms can sprout. From here you can recommend facilitators and board retreats; you can recommend reviewing the bylaws about establishing new policies, agenda formats, or other ideas that would improve the board. If you see structural changes you'd like to make, the governance committee is the place to start.

### Create a governance committee if you don't have one yet

If your board doesn't have a governance committee, suggest a "temporary" committee to tackle a governance issue, like reviewing the bylaws and recommending changes to the board. You could say, "I noticed when I read the board packet that the board hasn't revised its bylaws since 2002. I'd like to propose that a small group of people look through them and recommend any changes to the board for adoption."

Consider running the idea by a board leader first (such as the president or the president-elect) and then look for one or two reasonable members who could lend their perspective. Don't just choose other new board members, either. Someone who is a veteran of the board will be helpful for knowing what will fly with the board during discussion and also for swaying other board members later.

After the revision, once the board has had the chance to see how it went, the committee could be turned into a more permanent governance committee.

## Read the appendices of this book

There are appendices at the end of the book about revising bylaws, recruiting, and creating a strong committee structure. If you really want to get some nitty-gritty ideas for reforming the board, spend some time looking through them.

## Give this book away

It doesn't have to be this book, of course. (Although I would be honored if it were!) But if there's something you would like to improve, then you will likely be able to find an authoritative source recommending options to fix it. This book could be that, but so could an article or white paper from a variety of online resources like ForSmallNonprofits.com (the companion site for this book), BoardSource.org, 501commons.org, and other sites for nonprofits. It's a good idea to find "documentation" for the idea you're suggesting.

Suggest one fix

New board members have a period of time when they can suggest changes pretty much consequence-free. What might ruffle feathers after several years might be seen as a fresh new idea within your first few months on the board. But if you suggest a lot of radical changes all at once, you might scare some veteran board members. So pick one thing you'd like to fix and focus on that. Here are some practical improvements that could help your board.


If your board meetings are too long...

Alfred Hitchcock once said, "The length of a film should be directly related to the endurance of the human bladder." That goes for board meetings as well.

When I was the director of the Grand Cinema, the board meetings were marathon affairs lasting several hours. A meeting that starts at 5:30 and goes past 8:00 is really hard on board members and staff, especially after a full day of work. So I was pleasantly surprised that when I took my next job as an executive director, the board meetings were before a dinner meeting of the membership, so the meetings had a hard and fast end time. As a result, meetings went from 4:30 to 6:00 and no longer. Yes, some days it was 6:05 or 6:10, but going a few minutes long is different from running several hours. It was a real change of pace, and one I appreciated.

*Board meetings just don't need to take up a whole evening.*

If you need to reduce the length of your board meetings, I'd suggest setting a goal of keeping them less than two hours—but ideally closer to 90 minutes.

A goal is often not enough to keep people on track, though. So here's another suggestion: on the agenda include the end time for the meeting. Then, if the board meeting looks as if it will go over, request that someone make a motion to extend the meeting by 15 minutes.

If you have a string of marathon meetings, this will keep them much shorter. Even if you have to vote to extend the meeting that extra 15 minutes two or three times, the meetings will be shorter than if you didn't do so.

## If your board spends too long on one topic...

Board meetings will go more smoothly if the board adopts a general norm or practice that it will vote on a new policy at the meeting *after* the policy has been presented. That would mean that a new policy would be presented in March, let's say, where it is discussed and then sent back to the committee for further review. The policy would then come back to the board in April for a vote, whether or not it had been changed. This is a good norm. It allows a board time to give a policy a lot of thinking; it removes pressure to pass something that has just come before a board; and since it's a "norm" and not a policy, a board can choose not to follow it in times of emergency. It will also keep your board from spending a huge period of time on the issue at one meeting because you won't have to "fix" someone's objection on the fly. Take it back to the committee and present a revision at the next meeting. This will speed up the meeting and strengthen the work your committees does.

## If your board has conflict or fights...

Recommend an annual board retreat if there isn't one already. If there is an annual retreat, recommend that time be spent with a facilitator to talk about the issue dividing the board. Some people are afraid to let contentious issues out into the open, but a board retreat with a good facilitator should be a safe space for it.

A half-day board retreat will also allow the board to set the agenda for the year on the biggest topics it needs. A Saturday morning starting at 8:30 with a continental breakfast is a good start to a meeting. Ideally, the board retreat should be within the first three or four months of the fiscal year. If it's scheduled too early, you don't give incoming board members a chance to adjust their schedules. Too late, and too much of the year has gone by to be able to finish anything (or the work will be done by a new board that didn't have the buy-in at the retreat).

The day should be limited to a few core topics. I would also avoid starting with finances at these retreats. Board meetings are already full of finances. If you've gotten everyone together on a Saturday morning, it would be a waste to go over the budget again. Here's another way to think of it: the monthly finance reports are a way for the board to evaluate how the planning and strategizing that was done at a board retreat is proceeding.

If you have hired a facilitator for the meeting, your executive committee or governance committee should meet with the facilitator in advance to make sure the agenda and needs of the meeting are well defined. A good facilitator will have the experience needed to guide the board during the day's discussion.


If your board meets at night and has wine...

Some board members bring food and snacks to board meetings. This isn't a bad idea, unless it slows down the start of meetings or encourages meetings to go long because everyone is grazing and no one's stomach is rumbling and telling them it's time to go home. But board members probably shouldn't have a glass of wine or a beer during board meetings (even though it's not uncommon).

I know, I know, I'm a killjoy. But a board meeting is not for socializing, and a glass of wine is a sign that you can kick back a bit. It gets worse if one board member has one too many. Suddenly a whole new dynamic exists in the boardroom.

Think of it this way: if your executive director were pouring a glass of wine at 3:00 at work, how would you feel about that? Your work is just as important as hers. Your legal and fiduciary responsibilities should not be mixed with alcohol.

How to suggest this change? If you're new to the board, then *you're* going to be the killjoy. Frankly, it won't be easy. In fact, the easiest way to do it is to become the board president and just announce that you'd like the board not to have wine at the meetings. (It's easier to announce it than to ask for it from a junior position.)

One way to advocate for this is to focus on the distinction between work and social. Alcohol means social time, and your board is for working. Suggest that the bottle of wine be opened *after* the meeting. You can socialize a little more freely and maybe it will encourage people to speed up the meeting as well.

If your board members don't have strong relationships...

There are times when alcohol can be useful, such as when you want to have social occasions to help the board create an esprit de corps. Have an annual board holiday party or a summer barbecue. Whenever you choose to hold it, it's important for a board to socialize, and hopefully build social bonds that will form the basis for camaraderie and tighter relationships. This relationship building is important, but it's important to build it outside of the board meeting—or your meetings will become more social affairs than a place for work.

If your board has a bully...

A bully is one of the most toxic kinds of board members to have. Workplace bullying is a real thing, and it can happen on a board, too. It can be more insidious on a board because, frankly, there's not as much reason for a volunteer to put up with a bully. Bullied employees will continue to show up at work because they need the paycheck. A volunteer board member who feels bullied by another board member is much less likely to continue attending.

If you have a bully on your board, this is a collective problem that needs to be dealt with. Of course, "bully" is a loaded word. And maybe you are hesitant to call someone that —after all, we mostly think of bullying as a schoolyard issue, so calling someone a bully feels almost like calling them names or calling them a child.

But if you have someone whose behavior you would call "uncivil," "negative" or "disrespectful"... if you talk about someone being a "difficult person"... or that your board has a "personality conflict" you might be describing the effects of a bully.

I found these terms at workplacebullying.org, a useful site if you think you might have a problem with bullying. If you are unsure, check out that site or Google "workplace bullying." The ideas for dealing with it may not sound pleasant, because they almost all involve confrontation of the bully in some manner, but dealing with the problem is better than letting someone (or everyone) continue to be bullied by a member or two.

Remember... real change is slow

If you want to make changes to your board, know that real change is often slow. If you come onto a board and see a number of things you think should be improved, you're probably not going to get it all done in the first year.

As the proverb goes: *If you want to go quickly, go alone; if you want to go far, go together.*

You need to make changes at the pace of the board, which may be slower than you'd like. But if you keep at it, over time you will look back and see how far you've come.

## Step up

If you want to really change a board culture for the better, you're eventually going to have to consider stepping into some kind of leadership role, possibly a committee chair or one of the officer positions.

In numerous small ways, board culture is affected by how the leaders of the board behave and run the meeting. The final section of this book is on board leadership to address how that can happen.

FIVE

# BEING ON A BOARD WHEN THERE IS
## NO EXECUTIVE DIRECTOR

AT SOME VERY SMALL NONPROFITS, staff might consist solely of a bookkeeper or an administrative assistant, or there may not be paid staff at all. It may feel like a big chore to do all the work of board building described here, *plus* run the regular operations of the nonprofit. That's not uncommon.

Look for ideas in these pages that would directly help you in the most practical sense—maybe ideas for improving your meetings, implementing terms, and standardizing your committees. After that, you can set your sights higher if you choose to do so.

*And you don't have to do it.*

As I said earlier in this book, if you are a band of volunteers, and are perfectly content to remain that way, a lot of this may not apply. *A board structure and of these policies we've been talking about are designed to keep the nonprofit healthy over many years.* The structure, while it may seem complex or cumbersome, is what provides the ability for an organization to endure beyond the initial burst of enthusiasm from its volunteers. These policies and structures create the system that will help a board and the nonprofit it oversees to endure for the long term, even when the original founding members have moved on.

Without those structures, a nonprofit might last for a while, but the board (and thus the nonprofit) will likely be relying on the hard work of one or two board volunteers to keep things going. You will likely also find it more difficult to compete for grants without some of these structures in place.

It's OK if you don't want to go this direction. Stay small! Let your band of volunteers go out, achieve its mission, and then close up, its work complete.

But if you want to make your organization last longer than the time you're putting your individual energy into it, then you're going to want to begin building a board structure and improving your board.

## Separate board meetings from "working" meetings

If your goal is to improve the board structure while doing the regular business of your nonprofit, things are going to get busy. It might get hard to do both at the same time.

One idea to make this clearer is to separate "board" meetings from "working" meetings. Try alternating your meetings. In January schedule a board meeting to talk about budget, policy, and nominations. Then in February, schedule a working meeting where you plan the work needed to run your organization. If that's too much time away from the work, schedule quarterly "board" meetings, with the rest for working meetings. However you manage it, the idea of separating board governance from the work will help your board better understand when you have different roles.

Use technology to communicate about work...

...But do the work of the board in person. You can plan a lot over email or through Facebook groups. But it's harder to talk policy. Similar to the idea above, splitting up how you communicate about work will add more clarity to the shifting roles.

Appoint a volunteer executive director

Another option is to "hire" a volunteer executive director either from your board or from the community. This distinction makes it clearer where responsibilities lie and set the board up for growing successfully later—when hopefully it can pay someone in the position.

If the volunteer executive director is appointed from the board, that person should not remain on the board. The director should serve his or her role and the board should serve its role. The clarity is important.

A short job description is probably in order. This doesn't need to be a "classic" job description that states all the obvious points of what the position entails. Instead a description that defines some short-term goals and priorities is probably enough.

A board with a volunteer executive director will need to have flexible expectations for its "employee." As long as the mission is being furthered and the executive director is not damaging the brand or health of the nonprofit, then it's probably not a good idea to issue a reprimand for not fully understanding Microsoft Excel. This director is a volunteer. If he or she is making a sincere effort, let it go.

As with board term limits, I'd suggest that a term of commitment will help this relationship end well. Ask the volunteer executive director to hold the position for six months. If things are working smoothly, go for another six months. If the person is burned out and isn't able to continue, then everyone can part friends. Again, the defined commitment gives everyone a way to end it with grace.

## How to raise money to hire your first executive director

If you don't have an executive director, but want to hire one, here is a sample plan to hire your first executive director.

### First year

- The board commits to the idea of hiring an executive director as part of its strategic planning process.
- The board president or fundraising chair asks each board member to commit to a three-year "stretch" giving goal to help raise funds for the nonprofit.
- At least half of the funds from the annual fundraising event are saved, along with the stretch donations by the board.

### Second year

- At least 75 percent of the revenue from the annual fundraising event is saved, along with the second year of stretch donations by the board.
- Based on the pledges and the current state of the reserves from these savings, a rough salary is laid out for the position.
- Let's say a board saved $30,000 this way. (Between

a large percentage of the two fundraising events and two years of stretch board gifts, this shouldn't be a terribly high number, but your number might be smaller. That's fine.) Whatever the number is, it represents the upper limit of what a board can pay the executive director for the next year.

- The board then advertises for a part-time executive director. Let's say, using the above example, the board advertises for a position that is 20 hours per week for $20/hour. Total annual salary: about $20,800 (remember there will be other expenses beyond that, including state taxes and payroll fees).

- Please note, *of course* it's not as much as you would like to pay an executive director. For a parent returning to the workforce after a few years away, though, the flexibility might be just what they need. For a young person dedicated to your cause, it might be just the job they could use to make new connections. Even if *you* can't see yourself taking the job, that doesn't mean it's not a great fit for someone else.

- With careful hiring, and by demonstrating that you are committed to improving the quality of your board, you can attract someone with decent fundraising or other nonprofit qualifications. A paid staff member should have a good chance of successfully building new revenue that would have required too much time of the board.

*Third year*

- All the revenue from the annual fundraising event goes toward the salary of the executive director. Continuing from our current example, a fundraising breakfast, after three years of growth, should be able to raise a significant portion of that salary, if not all of it.

———

To be clear: My suggestion to use the annual fundraising event to pay for the executive director is a *budgeting* tool to help you establish a range for what you might be able to pay. You won't be telling your donors at the event that you are raising money for a new executive director. Because really... you aren't. You are *still* raising money for your mission. The board has identified that a strategic way to fulfill your mission is to hire an executive director. It's not as if the money is going straight from the event into the pocket of the executive director, or that if the event makes more than expected the executive director gets more.

The outside world should see your nonprofit doing more and more, even as you save for an executive director. Donations through the annual fund, revenue from membership (if that applies), grants, and more should all be growing (especially if you are following strategies in *The Little Book of Gold: Fundraising for Small and Very Small Nonprofits*). You shouldn't hear too many complaints that your donations are going to "administration."

As a side note, maybe you've heard about nonprofits that separate "administration" from "program." This can be useful for a fundraising ask ("all of your donations today go toward programs") or for grants, which might ask—or mandate—how much of the grant will go to administration.

The truth is that for small and very small nonprofits, the distinction isn't that meaningful. If you are a very small nonprofit that is growing into a small one, your staff is doing "program" work most of the time. The distinction between administration and program is much more meaningful for larger organizations.

If you are looking for a paid executive director for your organization, this simple model should get you the funding in place to hire someone within 24 months of the time you make the decision.

# PART TWO

# HOW TO BE A BOARD LEADER

After serving on the board, you may eventually be called upon to take a leadership role. I highly recommend stepping up if you like the work of the board. Your experience as a board member will be improved with the new position, you will have a bigger impact on the organization than you would have otherwise, and your personal relationships with other board members will deepen. If you're going to be on a board, I think you'll find that some of the more rewarding experiences come after a year or two when you step up as a leader. The following chapters deal with the responsibilities of committee chairs and the officers of the board.

# SIX

# HOW TO BE AN OFFICER OF THE BOARD

LEADERSHIP of the board is about more than the board president (a role that's big enough that I've dedicated the entire next chapter to it). A variety of leadership roles are available, depending on your talents, time availability, and interests.

We'll cover the main ones here.

### How to be president-elect

Many organizations have an office of either president-elect or vice president, which generally mean the same thing—the person most likely to be president next term. (If there is any difference between the two titles, I'd say that the title "president-elect" means that the officeholder has already agreed to be the next president, while the title "vice president" only *suggests* the leadership succession.)

Whichever title your board uses, the role should be a place for likely future presidents to get their feet wet. President-elects should be included in all executive committee meetings, should be in close contact with the president, and stand in for the president when he or she is not available.

I recommend that the president-elect serve on the governance or nominations committee. Those are great places to learn the ins and outs of an organization's structure.

Other than that, the job of the president-elect is to soak it all in and learn as much as possible from the board and staff. It can help make the transition to president easier.

## How to be past president

If the job of president-elect is to learn what it means to be president, the job of past president is to learn what it means to let go. Once you've stepped down from the presidency, your job is to be called upon *when asked* and go back to being an ordinary everyday board member the rest of the time.

Resist the temptation to give advice that starts with "When I was president..." You did your job, and hopefully you did it well. Maybe you feel that the new president has a lot to learn. If so, give the person space to learn it, or wait for him or her to come to you before you offer help. Trying to foist your experience on someone who doesn't want it just isn't going to work.

## How to be treasurer

The job of treasurer is twofold.

The first job is to understand the monthly finances of the nonprofit at an elemental level and look for early warning signs. What drives revenue? What drives expenses? Is a bad month merely a bad month? Or is there something bigger at work? Is there something about the profit and loss statement that looks odd? Answering these questions to your own satisfaction is of primary importance.

That's because the second job of the treasurer is to accurately convey the information in the reports to the rest of the board. Yes, everyone should be reading the reports and asking questions and forming their own opinions. But the treasurer is their guide. At the board meeting, the treasurer should highlight key trends in the report, make comments about anything substantially different from expectations, and then give a short conclusion.

Then the board members get to ask their questions. If the treasurer isn't certain of the correct answer, the executive director can certainly jump in. But the treasurer should do his or her best to be prepared.

What follows are the other key duties of the treasurer.


*Lead finance committee meetings.*

A finance committee meeting usually starts with the executive director presenting the most recent financials and answering questions—much like how the treasurer will go through them with the board later, but in much more depth.

After that, there is usually time for looking at other issues related to the organization's finances: maybe some business planning, budget development, bid comparisons for a new operational service, or committee work on cash-handling policies. A treasurer should be the leader of these meetings and the point person for keeping the committee on track, even if it's the executive director who is the one carrying out the majority of the work.


*Work with the executive director.*

During routine finance committee meetings, everyone should be on the same "side." Even if the report shows a loss, it should not be seen as a personal failure on the part of the executive director. The reason: presenting a profit and loss statement that shows a loss is already hard on an executive director. (I can speak from experience here—it's not fun to sit down at a finance committee meeting and show an unexpected loss of several thousand dollars, even if it's not your fault.)

If a treasurer compounds those feelings with personal attacks or passive-aggressive remarks about the performance of the executive director, this is creating an environment that can lead an executive director to make a dumb decision—like manipulating the numbers to create a better monthly report.

The executive director should not be afraid to show the finances to the board. The numbers are the numbers. Deal only with the numbers at the finance committee, not the executive director's performance. A treasurer should use the meeting to understand the profit and loss statement and balance sheet as well as possible and, with the rest of the committee, look for solutions to correcting any issues, if needed.

Everyone is on the same team.


*Research unusual financial questions.*

A gala fundraiser was packed, but the revenue seems light. There is a check written to a company the treasurer doesn't recognize. There is a call from a donor who says his donation check shows it was deposited into an account with a different name. There is a surprisingly high rate of churn through petty cash. The cash register is off by several hundred dollars over the course of the month. There are expenses on the bank statement that don't appear in the books.

All of these should be cause for the treasurer to dig deeper. Most of the time, it's probably an innocent explanation. Sometimes, this research will uncover mistakes that the finance committee will need to address, through either new policies or new procedures. On a rare occasion, the treasurer will uncover petty theft or wholesale embezzlement by a volunteer, staff member, or the executive director.

The treasurer's job is to get to the bottom of these unusual financial questions when they arise. Again, most of the time it's nothing. But a treasurer needs to be paying attention.

*Sound the alarm.*

The treasurer is likely the first board member who will see if something is *truly* going wrong with the finances. In those scenarios, the treasurer has a duty to alert the board president, the executive committee, or the full board as soon as possible. It's not a problem just for the treasurer, and sometimes it's not a problem that can wait a few weeks for a board meeting. If you see that the organization is heading for a huge financial cliff, pick up the phone and alert the board president immediately.

## How to be secretary

The secretary of the board is an under-appreciated role. We'll start with the most common—and frequently *only*—task of the job. But there's a lot more a secretary can do than just take minutes.

*Take minutes.*

Being secretary of the board means that one of your key duties is taking minutes and then typing them up. For as dry as it sounds, it's incredibly important. If there are no minutes of a board meeting, then it may as well have not happened. With no records of your votes, then how do you know what was passed?

How do you know what the motion said? Anyone with cause to question your board's decisions will find it very easy to make their case *because there is no record to support you.*

A secretary needs to make sure to record the minutes (or arrange for a staff member to do so) and have them approved by the board at the next meeting.

Just what are in the minutes exactly? Date, time, location, and a list of the board members who are present. A list of discussion topics, the specific wording of motions, and the tallies of votes on each motion, if it wasn't a unanimous vote.

What's not in the minutes? A point-by-point recap of every discussion. Instead of writing paragraphs about the two sides in a disagreement over a new policy, a simple one-sentence summary is fine. Minutes should primarily contain the business enacted and a list of discussion topics. They don't have to be much more than that.

*Know the bylaws.*

A secretary should have a copy of the bylaws handy at meetings. How many people make a quorum? What do the bylaws say about appointing a new board member in the middle of a term? How much notice do we have to give before the annual meeting? The secretary should be ready to answer.

*Confirm the legal status of the nonprofit.*

A secretary should be the one board member who wants to confirm every pesky detail. Do we still have our original 501(c)(3) letter? When is our business license due? When is our registration with the state due? It's a small duty, and you can generally count on your executive director to take care of these questions. But it's the board secretary who should make sure it has happened.

*Gather other important documents.*

If your board has a conflict of interest policy or a memorandum of understanding that you ask all members to sign every year, who gathers those documents? Who emails a board member who hasn't done it yet? It should be the secretary who keeps track of the board's responsibilities to each other, not the executive director (even if the documents eventually go to the executive director to be housed in the office).

*One small note about the position of secretary*

There's no other way to say this, so I'll be blunt. The title "secretary" seems to scare off men. It's as if they're afraid that if they are secretary they'll have to start wearing a pencil skirt and get drinks for the board president like they're Peggy Olson on the first season of *Mad Men*.

I want to see women in more leadership positions on boards, but I'm also tired of seeing men treat this position as if it's beneath them—as if only a woman can fill this role. On all the boards I've served on (or served for), there was only one that had a male secretary, and then just for one year.

(Next time the secretary is absent from your board meeting and the president asks for a volunteer to fill in, notice who volunteers and who doesn't. I'll bet you anything that it's not a man volunteering.)

Guys, step it up. There is nothing emasculating about taking minutes.

How to be a committee chair

Running a committee of the board is like being the chair of a mini-board. The duties are similar:

- To work with the members of the committee to set a regular meeting date and time.
- To work with the executive director to get the information needed for the committee's work.
- To write and distribute the agenda for the committee's meetings.
- To lead meetings.
- And finally, to represent the committee at the full board meeting.

———

Those are the most common leadership positions of the board. Your nonprofit might have slightly different titles, but most likely, the core duties are those listed above.

The next and last chapter is about being board president.

# SEVEN

# HOW TO BE BOARD PRESIDENT

THE ROLE of board president or board chair will be different depending on the particular needs of your nonprofit and its staff. But there are some common themes among all of them. We'll go over some of those common tasks soon, but first, it's important to look at the big picture before we get into those details.

## Why be board president?

All too often, a nonprofit board gets close to the end of its fiscal year, and no one is willing to step up to become the next president. People see more work and more headaches and they think, Why would I sign up for that?

It *is* more work, but it doesn't have to mean more headaches. There are a lot of good reasons you might want to think of standing for election to be board president.

*Influencing the path of the nonprofit*

A board president is in a better position to influence the direction of the nonprofit and how it lives out its mission. That *isn't* to say that board presidents get their way. In fact, the job requires a lot of listening to what *others* want for the nonprofit. But in several small ways, the job will allow you a bigger voice about the direction of the organization, should you want it. (And if you *do* want it, and get it, please don't abuse it.)

*Personal fulfillment*

Stepping up to this kind of leadership role in a volunteer capacity can be very fulfilling. You obviously care about the mission of the organization—otherwise you wouldn't be on the board. As president, you can be a steward of the organization in a very active and meaningful way.

The experience is, without a doubt, rewarding. You will stretch muscles you didn't know you had; you will build a closer relationship with the executive director and your fellow board members than you would have otherwise; and you will step down from office in a year or two knowing you have done your best to guide the ship. If you have a day job that doesn't make you feel that you're saving the planet and the people who live on it (or whatever your particular passion is) this is a really good opportunity to get that sense of accomplishment and satisfaction.

*Personal recognition*

Along with the personal fulfillment comes the possibility for personal recognition among your peers and the wider community. There's nothing wrong with acknowledging that the role of board president means you are the one to stand up in front of meetings and to address the crowd at the fundraising breakfast. If your business or your career would benefit from having that recognition, those side benefits of the role might have some appeal.

The caution I have for you is that sometimes the job demands being unpopular. Just as a favorite teacher is often strict, a good board president will be called upon to lay down the law from time to time. Everyone is counting on you to be the one to rap the board on the knuckles when they need it, or to be the public face of the organization about a painful 30 percent budget cut.

Personal recognition is fine, but your desire for it shouldn't outweigh the work that needs to be done.

*Do it because you can, because the nonprofit needs you*

If you have taken the time to read this book, you probably know more about boards and nonprofits than many currently-serving board presidents. Really. Your willingness to pick up a book to become a better board member or to get ideas for improving your board makes you stand out. Maybe you are feeling that everyone else on your board knows more than you do, but that's certainly not true where it counts.

Yes, some members may have more history with the organization than you do. But after a year or two of serving on a board, no matter how it *feels*, you are probably just as ready as the current president. Don't let fear hold you back.

If you can do it, you should consider it. Your nonprofit needs you.

———

So what are the common duties of a board president? We'll go through them now.

.  .  .

*Public speaking*

I thought I would put the scary one first. Yes, the board president will be called upon to speak at a fundraising breakfast, at a membership meeting, upon receiving an award, or at some other public event.

One of the board presidents I served under was terrified of public speaking before he took the job, but with practice he got much better. He quoted a phrase he'd heard that I thought was apt—"it's not about getting rid of the butterflies in your stomach, it's about getting them to fly in formation."

You'll likely just have to get used to the butterflies. I speak in public all the time because of my elected position and I still get some butterflies before I go on. Practice is the only cure for fear of public speaking.

If you really want to be board president, but are truly scared of public speaking, don't let this stand in your way. Another board member or the executive director can speak in settings when this is needed, and it won't be an issue. If you want to lead, this does not have to be required.


*Preparing the board meeting agenda*

I recommend that the board president have an active hand in preparing the agenda. Usually this should be done with assistance from committee chairs and the executive director. Two weeks before the board meeting, send an email asking what people have for the agenda. You might already have a good idea, but this will give you a sense of the total scope (how much is on it, whether something needs to be bumped, etc.). You should have it ready to be sent out a week before the meeting.

If your time is short, you can work with the executive

director on this. But don't delegate this task exclusively to the ED. It's the *board's* meeting, not the director's.

*Leading board meetings*

As board president, you will generally be expected to lead the meeting. This means the decision to start the meeting on time is up to you, and ending it at a reasonable time is likely within your power, too. This might take a firm hand at first, but then it should get easier.

During the board meeting itself, you are the most likely person to keep the meeting on track. If someone has gone off-topic or goes over their allotted time, you're the one who can jump in without ruffling too many feathers.

It's a tricky balance of calling board members back to the topic or cutting them off—you don't want to slap someone down in front of their fellow board members, but you also need to establish that things need to stay on topic.

If someone is running long, jump in when they take a breath with, "I really hate to cut you off, Bob, but we're starting to sneak into the time allotted for strategic planning. Do you need a vote from the board tonight or can we pick this back up at the next meeting?"

If someone is off-topic, again you're going to have to jump in. "Dennis, I need to jump in real quick. I agree, those are good questions we'd like to know about our demographics, but I want to make sure we don't get too far off from the agenda item on the table. Alison, as the marketing committee chair, can you take up the question of demographics at a future committee meeting and go through what we know and what we don't?"

(Board presidents should often refer ideas to committees and let the collective wisdom of the group run with an idea. In the case of a bad idea, the committee can find the kernel that does work or gently let the board member down. For the board president this relieves the burden of being a focal point for every board member's pet ideas or suggestions. By referring it to a committee, other board members can jointly share the responsibility of hearing out ideas.)

Maybe the idea of interrupting someone feels rude to you. I get that. But you are the person that people are looking to for guidance when someone needs to be interrupted (and yes, sometimes people do *need* to be interrupted). Think of yourself as the voice of what everyone else is thinking. You can also think about it this way: your title as board president is a sort of armor that allows you to jump in where otherwise it might be considered rude. As long as you do so respectfully, people will understand that you are trying to keep the meeting on track, simply because of your title.

As with all possible jobs of the board president, you don't have to do them all. If you really don't think you can jump in and cut someone off in mid-speech, that's OK. But you should recognize that *someone* needs that job. You could ask the board secretary to do it, and then tell the board that the secretary will be keeping an eye on time and jumping in if needed. (Telling the board is important, because it means that they are expecting it and the "armor" of the title is transferring to the secretary.)

Here's another idea: empower other board members. Buy two of those really big foam hands that people take to football games and give them to two of your quieter board members. Tell the board that these two have the task of keeping the board on topic. Whenever someone delves too far off-topic, or does for too long, they wave the bright foam hand.

The silliness of it, and the fact that it's a visual reminder and not someone jumping in and interrupting the speaker, means this can get the meeting back on track without making the speaker feel *too* bad.

———

The job of leading the meetings is most important during times of real debate and differences of opinion on the board. As a board member, you get to have an opinion and a vote, of course. But you are also the one who needs to make sure the debate is productive, and doesn't just veer into chaos.

For example, if during an argument, two people try to talk at the same time, you can say, "Karen, then Jerry next." With just that, you've established that you're moderating. Almost certainly, the next person who wants to talk will catch your eye and lift a hand. You just have to nod at them, and then when Jerry's done you say, "Dennis, you had something you wanted to add?" If someone tries to supersede Dennis, you do the same thing as you did with Karen and Jerry—bump them. "Sorry, Alison, Dennis was next. Then you." This keeps any one or two people from monopolizing the discussion too much.

You also have an opportunity—if not the duty—to call on someone who hasn't said anything. "Barb, we haven't heard from you. What's your take?" This small offering is a good way to make sure that opposite views are being aired. If Barb declines, that's fine. But the offer to a silent board member— especially if her body language is tense or shows disagreement— should be made when the discussion is important.

### Listening to your board members

One of the most important jobs of the board president is listening to other board members.

Get to know them as people. Ask them why they wanted to be on the board and where they'd like to see the nonprofit in five years. Ask them how they think things have been going, and if they have any suggestions for things they'd like to see changed on the board. If they have a concern, tell them they should reach out to you. It's important to have a good sense of where the board is, especially when there are big decisions in front of the board.

It's important, too, to remember that listening to what board members says doesn't necessarily mean acting on everything they say. That would make you a reactionary president, pulled in all directions. Pay attention to your gut—is what the board member asking for a good idea? Do you think the idea is a good one? Is it relatively painless, even if you don't agree?

Also, pay attention *especially* when you hear the same thing from more than one person. Maybe someone is a little upset about a behavior of the executive director. That doesn't mean you need to go off trying to correct it. But if you hear of someone else concerned, it's time to start paying closer attention. Either someone on the board is trying to stir the pot and get people on their side, or the behavior of the executive director might need to be corrected. Good relationships with board members will mean that these discussions won't blindside you too often.

## Some thoughts on dealing with board members who monopolize your time

As with many jobs of the board president, listening to board members can be a delicate balance. You want them to feel heard, but you don't want—and can't afford—to spend hours and hours of your time in one-on-one coffee meetings or on endless phone calls with the board. All board presidents struggle with this balance.

You should be willing to takes calls and coffee meetings with your fellow board members, but I would suggest that these take place on your terms. If evenings are hard for you to spend an hour on the phone because you want to spend time with your family, then simply don't do it. Suggest talking during the day or early morning. If coffee meetings are hard for you to make time for because of the time to travel to the coffee shop, then suggest in-person meetings at your office or home. Whatever it is, make it work for *your* schedule. It's easy to think like an employee and want to say yes as often as you can to your board members. But you represent board members and should lead them. You don't work for them. Make time for them in the way that's easiest for you.

That said, the old 80/20 rule probably applies here. 80 percent of the calls and requests on your time are going to come from 20 percent of your board. Many board members simply won't think to call the board president about an issue and will deal with something on their own, through the committee process, or just let it go. But for some board members, calling the board president will be their first response.

Sometimes this can be a good thing—you don't want someone causing a ruckus or getting out way ahead of the board. But there just aren't many things that board members should be doing on their own that would allow them to get way ahead of the board as a whole.

In my experience, someone who asks for more and more of the board president's time is probably either venting about a personality conflict or trying to do an end-run around a committee's work to get their own way. Common topics for calls might be: the executive director isn't listening to my ideas; I have a great marketing strategy that should be implemented immediately but the committee said no; I think we're making a big mistake with the location for this year's breakfast; I'm upset that no one is signing up to be table captains; Jerry was rude to me...

These kinds of repeated calls from a board member can be difficult and can end up making a lot of work for everyone—the board president, and all the people (staff and other board members) whom the board president is calling upon to deal with the persistent caller.

It's up to you to protect your own time and keep your focus on the *entire* board, not just on dealing with one or two very vocal members.

The important thing to remember is that (most of the time) it is not up to you to solve the problems of every board member. Your position *does not* make you a parent of fourteen toddlers who need you to intercede on their behalf all the time. They are all adults and can work things out.

Dealing with board members who are trying to monopolize your time is hard. The easiest way to handle them is to divert them back into the board and committee structure:

*The executive director isn't listening to my ideas.*

"I know you feel passionately about this, but we have to give Linda the space to run the operations, within the guidelines of the budget and policy. I'd suggest bringing up your idea during the conversation about next year's budget if you feel that it's that important, and we'll see what the rest of the board thinks."

*I have a great marketing strategy that should be implemented immediately but the committee said no.*

"I know you feel very passionately about this, but the marketing committee knows how tightly we have our resources stretched. We can't implement every good idea, and we have to trust the marketing committee to keep us focused."

. . .

*I think we're making a big mistake with the location for this year's breakfast.*

"Why don't you join the fundraising committee at their next meeting and run your thoughts by them? If you can't make it, I'm sure the committee chair would want to hear your concerns."


*I'm upset that board members aren't signing up to be table captains for the fundraising breakfast.*

"I agree. You should bring it up at the next board meeting. I'll back you on it one hundred percent."


*Jerry was rude to me.*

"Why don't you give Jerry a call and talk it over with him? See if there's an issue that needs to be cleared up, or if it was something that was unintentional. If you both can't reach an understanding, the three of us can meet and we'll talk things over together."

———

If someone is monopolizing your time with repeated calls, emails, and questions, this is when a strong board and committee structure will reveal itself as an asset.

Here's what happens when you don't have that structure to rely on: the board president gets off the phone after an hour-long call with the disgruntled board member. He emails a committee chair or the executive director, relaying the frustration of that board member. Accommodations are suggested. Return calls are made. Things are changed to "fix" the situation.

In all, everyone has a lot of extra communication and extra

work to try to make the upset board member happy. Often this is done entirely behind the scenes, too. So decisions are made to please a board member that others aren't even aware of (and might be against, if they were privy to the conversation).

It's the kind of office politics that people hate at work—they shouldn't need to go through it in their volunteer time as well.

There are many reasons that some board members choose to go around the regular lines of committee work. It could be that some board members are shy and insecure in a group; it could be that they want to get their way no matter what it takes; it could be that the proper channels were never explained to them (that one's on you); or it could be that they don't know any different way of behaving.

Whatever the reason, look at the result: A single board member got you, the board president, (and possibly additional volunteers and staff) to respond to their frustration or complaint without having to advocate for that concern in an open session of the board or committee.

That grants a single board member *enormous* power. Why would they go through the messy, but important, work of the board and committee structure if they can get their way by working around it?

Some board members might not get the hint when you advise them to use the board structure, and you may need to be more direct about your needs and expectations. Here are some ideas:

- "I know this is important to you, but I just cannot give any more time to this right now. Why don't you see how things go for a while, and give me an update when I see you at the next board meeting?"
- "I appreciate your inviting me to join in this

discussion, but weighing in on this probably falls outside my role as president."

- "I need to focus on my family and my work and my other duties as board president. I just can't add this to my plate right now."

Many of these statements, while polite, might earn you a retort along the lines of—"But isn't taking care of this situation for me part of your job?"

Again, to be clear, it's not. You should not be spending hours and hours on the phone or in meetings because a single board member wants you to do so. A possible response:

"I don't think it is, but I guess we have different ideas on what the role of the board president is. Why don't I add it to the agenda at the end of the next board meeting and we'll see if I'm out of step with others on the board, too. Maybe we can all reach a consensus together."

This models an important behavior to your whole board: important topics should not be discussed only in the shadows.

In short:

- The board president does not answer to the beck and call of an individual board member, especially if individuals frequently ask for too much of your time.
- Refer board members who ask for too much of your time back into the committee and board structure to get them off your plate.
- When in doubt, get things out into the open quickly and moderate a discussion.

## Having hard conversations with board members

Another job of the board president is having hard—but necessary—conversations with board members. This could be about their poor attendance at meetings, their treatment of a staff member or fellow board member, their lack of giving, or a host of other topics. You're probably not going to like it, but the good news is, you probably don't have to do it that often.

If you have never been in a position in which you need to have a "corrective" conversation, here are a couple of tips that will help you get through it:

- *"Praise in public, and criticize in private."* A good proverb for dealing with volunteers. You probably shouldn't call someone out in front of the rest of the board unless there has been an immediate transgression that significantly crossed the line.
- *Emails are almost always misinterpreted.* Use the phone or meet in person.
- *Memorize your first line.* The first time I had to fire an employee, I used this mental trick to make sure that I didn't stumble all over myself trying to ease into giving bad news and end up saying nothing. So memorize the first sentence that you want to say. Once the Band-Aid has been ripped off, it's easier to have a productive conversation. It's actually helpful to the person you're talking to, as well, because he or she doesn't have to strain to understand what the topic is about just because you're afraid to get to the point.
- *Remember that the other board members or staff members are counting on you.* You are having the hard conversation because the other board members

are relying on you to do so. They are the ones being hurt by this board member's behavior. Keep them in mind.

- *After the discussion, remind the board member how glad you are to have them on the board.* Praise is best after a tough conversation, not before. (If you praise someone before the hard conversation, the next time you praise them, they can't help but wonder what's coming next.)

### Listening to your executive director

The relationship with your executive director should be strong. I like to think of it as the hinge on which the rest of the nonprofit functions. The two of you should have each other's backs. That doesn't mean you should have to agree on everything, but you should sort things out together, and (generally) act as a team.

In cases of real disagreement, there should be mutual respect and neither side should fight dirty while trying to advocate for their position. Along those lines, I would say that neither the board president nor the executive director should surprise the other in a meeting if they can possibly help it.

As an executive director, I generally tried to have weekly or twice-monthly meetings with my board president either over breakfast or coffee, or at the president's office. Sometimes there wasn't much to talk about, but it was good to have a strong foundation for our working relationship.

### Having hard conversations with your executive director

Despite the importance I place on this relationship and the need to build camaraderie, the board president is still the closest thing to a direct supervisor that the executive director has. That means that at times, the relationship is very much a supervisor/employee relationship.

Except... it's not. It's a unique dynamic: The supervisor doesn't work on site with the employee; the employee is paid, but the supervisor is not; the supervisor is representing not only their own opinion, but what they hear from other board members; and finally—the employee knows that if they wait a year or so, they'll probably get a new supervisor.

It's an unusual relationship in the employment world.

The executive director and board president should start their time together with a clear understanding of expectations and communication styles. But at some point, the president may have to have a hard conversation. Maybe requesting a behavior to be changed. Or directing, on behalf of the board, that a certain course be followed over the executive director's wishes. These can be hard conversations. But it's the job of the board president to have them. The same advice presented earlier on having hard conversations with board members applies to having them with the executive director as well.

### "To hire and fire"

As mentioned in the first chapter, the board is responsible for supervising the executive director, as well as hiring, evaluating, and terminating him or her. The board president almost always leads these processes. Here are some tips for managing each one.

### To hire, create a search committee.

Unless you have fewer than seven or so people on your board, you shouldn't attempt to hire an executive director at the board level. The best plan is to create a search committee to manage the process on the board's behalf. This should be a small group, but it should ask for input early from the whole board. (If you have a president-elect or a vice president who is expected to become president, this is a great committee for them to lead, since they'll end up working closely with the new hire, likely even more than the current board president.)

The search committee should seek input on the qualities and skills other board members are looking for in an executive director. It should also seek board approval of a job description and salary range for the position as early as possible. That committee should also inform the board of its hiring plan: where it will post the job, the process for board members to suggest candidates, the process candidates will use to apply, and the interview process the hiring committee will use. This is to prevent surprises later.

After that, the search committee should manage the hiring process until it is ready to recommend a candidate.

There are a few ways of handling this. As I said, when I was hired at the Grand Cinema, my final interview was with the full board of seventeen members. The board also interviewed two other candidates and then made its decision. That is a lot of work to expect of seventeen people.

For a polar opposite example, when I was hired to be the executive director of another nonprofit, the search committee made its recommendation to the board via email, and I was hired by an email vote without many members having even met me.

Ideally, a search committee should return to the full board with one, *maybe* two candidates, but only if it's a small board. To ask a large board to weigh the relative strengths of two reasonably qualified candidates all but guarantees that the meeting will last long into the night. Don't put them through it.

In short, the larger the board, the more it should rely on the search committee.

*For personnel complaints, rely on the executive committee.*

You see this in the work world sometimes: employees who don't like a decision of their boss take an issue to their boss's boss. It's tricky enough in the work world to handle this appropriately, but it's even trickier when "the boss's boss" is a board of fifteen. How should a board handle complaints from staff below the executive director?

First, employees who are dissatisfied with the business or operational choices of their boss, the executive director, should generally not get a hearing from the board, or even the executive committee. The board has hired the executive director to carry out operations, and the board should rely on him or her to do it. It's only natural to expect that every employee won't agree with every decision the director makes.

But an employee who comes to a board member with a *personnel* complaint about the executive director—harassment of any kind, discrimination, and the like—should be taken very seriously by the board.

Board members who hear about something like this from an employee of the executive director have a responsibility to pass it along to the board president to be handled by the executive committee, and maybe eventually the full board. Individual board members should not attempt to deal with it on their own, and they should not keep the secret of the employee. (They should also not expect to continue to have inside information about the process just because the employee came to them first.)

For the most serious of complaints from employees about fraud, illegal activity, or more by the executive director, a board should implement a "whistleblower" policy to protect those staff members who come forward.


*To evaluate, rely on the executive committee.*

Hardly anyone enjoys personnel evaluations, either the person giving them or the person receiving them. Evaluating an executive director as a board is often even more challenging. Sometimes a board member may see the executive director only once a month. It's not a solid basis for issuing an insightful evaluation. As a result, individual board members should likely not be sitting across from the executive director and offering performance feedback unless they are on the leadership of the board.

The process of evaluating the executive director should be managed by the board president and the executive committee.

As with many things, I recommend keeping it practical and easy.

One option is to do away with the formal evaluation and rely on the board president or Executive Committee to give feedback on the spot. It has its own set of pitfalls—what if no feedback is being given to the executive director? But it's a system worth considering at small nonprofits, where there is frequent contact between the board and the executive director.

Here's a more conscious plan of evaluating an executive director: the board president can ask board members three questions. "What should the executive director keep doing? What should she start doing? What should she stop doing?" Then the board president assembles the most frequent responses and presents them to the executive director. Clear and to the point.

Whatever your system of evaluation as a board, there are some practical ways to make the process go more smoothly.

First, on serious issues, don't wait until the evaluation to bring it up. There should be no surprises on an evaluation, and there shouldn't be much "old business." Telling someone they really screwed up eight months ago isn't useful to anyone. The board president or the executive committee should deal with these issues when they happen.

Second, use the executive committee or the president as a filter. Not every random comment from a board member needs to be passed on to the executive director. A small group meeting is best for delivering a clear message to an employee. Too many cooks in the kitchen can confuse the issue.

Third, avoid overly bureaucratic solutions. Board members who have been in corporate, academic, or government positions often have a hard time imagining that the solutions that work in their world may not translate to a small organization. But simple plans are ideal for a small nonprofit. If your evaluation is nothing more than a meeting between the executive director and the executive committee talking about how things are going, that's fine. Go with it.

*To fire your executive director...*

... I hope you never have to fire an executive director. Or "let them go." Or "terminate their employment." All of these terms get to the same act: releasing an executive director from employment before the person wants to go. I appreciate the clarity of "fire," though, so that's the term I'm going to use in this section.

There's a lot to cover on this topic, but let's start with the basics before we get to the nuance. For what reasons might you even consider firing an executive director? I'm ordering this list from the most objective reasons to the most subjective.

*When the director has stolen money from the nonprofit.*

This should be obvious, and it's almost certainly not worth allowing a second chance.

*When the director has broken the law, especially as it relates to hiring practices (such as discrimination in hiring) or other actions that might open the nonprofit up to legal liability.*

Again, this should be pretty obvious. "He said, she said" cases are harder to evaluate as a board, where the truth of the alleged action is unclear. Legal counsel can advise the board on recommended courses of action.

*When the director has made a serious mistake, was formally asked by the board to correct the error, and failed to do so or repeated the serious mistake again.*

The word "serious" is important in that sentence. This might mean breaking a code of ethics that has been previously established, or it might be a singular incident that there's no policy for—the executive director may have just had a singularly bad screw-up of some kind.

One mistake—a truly colossal error that endangered the nonprofit's viability, possibly in a public way—might be grounds for immediate dismissal. But most of the time, there's room to ask for an error to be corrected, and for the executive director to repair any broken trust with the board.

How the executive director addresses his or her error is of utmost importance. An executive director who has made a serious mistake and refuses to acknowledge it or apologize for it may not get a second chance. One who admits it, apologizes, and expresses willingness to work with the board to repair the relationship might get that chance.

.  .  .

*When the director demonstrates repeated inability to perform the tasks of the job.*

Repeatedly not bringing promised documents to a board meeting; repeatedly missing important deadlines; repeatedly losing major gifts from good donors. How many times is repeated? How many donors can you afford to lose? How many missed meetings are too many? These are subjective assessments, but they are important assessments. You shouldn't be continually making excuses for an executive director, especially if the objectives or financial needs of the nonprofit are starting to suffer.

*When the director shows an inability to lead through a time of major transition.*

This is really tricky, but let's say that the work of a board has led to the adoption of a strategic plan that would create real upheaval in the work of the nonprofit and push it in a new direction. The transition, or the new needs of the organization, may take a certain set of skills that your executive director doesn't possess. The director had the skills to do the last job, but not this one. Do you offer training? Could the director hire others who have the needed skills? Or do you *truly* need new leadership? This is all subjective, of course, but in this scenario a board may arrive at the conclusion that it needs to make a change.

———

Having listed the reasons above, it's now time for me to walk it back.

While I believe the reasons listed can be valid, you should know that it is rare for a nonprofit to fire its executive director.

Nine times out of ten—and this is especially true with small nonprofits—a nonprofit board just doesn't want to pull the trigger.

There are structural reasons for this reluctance. One of them is that it's often hard to get a group of people onto the same page about something that is such a big deal. People bring to the board their own mixture of feelings about employment and what it means to fire people. Maybe some board members have been fired themselves and wouldn't want to put anyone through it. Maybe some members work at large institutions where firing someone means an exercise in documentation and leaving a paper trail that the nonprofit doesn't have. Maybe some simply like the executive director.

Some nonprofit board members just don't know enough to decide whether the director should be fired or not. If they see the executive director at a board meeting and a committee meeting twice a month, is that enough information to go on to make a decision? Some board members won't feel it is.

There's also a tendency for board members at small nonprofits to want to give the benefit of the doubt to their executive director, and offer them another chance.

And finally: in a small nonprofit with just a handful of employees, the person who was fired might take some time to replace... and who's going to do all their work in the meantime?

Getting a diverse group of people to agree about this means that firing a nonprofit executive director is uncommon.

On the other hand, when executive directors *are* fired, it's not always for the best of reasons. Sometimes the reasons are about internal politics, personal grudges, or other things that are unrelated to the performance of the executive director or the performance of the nonprofit as a whole.

I definitely take note when an executive director in my town leaves a position suddenly (and doesn't have another job lined up). If the nonprofit is an outwardly healthy-looking organization, I wonder what the real story was behind the termination. Sometimes I know the individual and they've told me their side of the story afterward, blaming one or two board members that drove them out.

Is that an excuse? Am I just hearing their side of the story? I'm hard-pressed to say for sure, but you should be aware of my personal bias here. As someone who has worked twice as a director, barring all other information I probably lean a bit more toward the executive director's side than the board's side.

I've seen how a bully on a board can stir up enough of a tempest to get an executive director fired. I've seen how a board can find itself trapped in a certain internal logic that makes firing an executive director *seem* like the only option.

It's the chance that this can happen that makes me so cautious as I write this section about "when a board should fire an executive director." I list these reasons for you, the board president, because if there is a fraught relationship between the board and the staff, you may start hearing calls for this kind of drastic action. Do your best to ask that board members not discuss this with one another casually. Emphasize that it's a really big deal and that if a board member really wants to discuss the performance of the executive director, that person should call for an executive session at the end of a board meeting to discuss the topic as a full board.

If there is evident support for firing your executive director, I recommend the same course of action that I do for other policies coming to the board: take a little time. An executive committee can study a situation in-depth and bring back a recommendation to the board. That could be a recommendation for discipline, corrective action, and moving forward with the relationship or it could be a recommendation for termination. That extra time for a small group to look at this important decision will help guard against any mob mentality that might have been forming.

Again, it's rare for a board to have to go through this, so hopefully you won't have to crack open this section again. On to happier duties!

### Making nice when needed

A board president is often useful to patch up relationships the organization has with customers, vendors, or partner organizations. As an executive director, I can remember several times when someone was upset at either me personally or the organization as a whole. While I often could defuse the situation, I called in the board president when I couldn't.

Just talking to the highest possible "authority," and having their problem heard and understood is often all someone needs. It may be enough to simply promise that you'll have a conversation with your executive director about the matter. Alternatively, a board president can offer a year's extension of their membership, a refund, or some other small token of apology that might not have been accepted coming from the executive director.

One thing to keep in mind: if someone cares enough to complain all the way up the line to the board president, they are likely a strong supporter of your organization (when they're not upset at you, that is). *Do* spend the time to try to make things right. You may find later that you're glad you did.

### Signing checks

Both boards that I've worked for have had a threshold: checks above a certain amount need two signatures. This prevents the executive director from writing a fantastically large check to herself and running off to Venezuela.

In these cases, one board member, and sometimes two, will be asked to be registered with the bank as a signer on checks. I recommend the president and another officer—maybe the secretary or the president-elect. Ideally, it shouldn't be the treasurer. Some nonprofits give the treasurer signing power because it has to do with money—"treasurers deal with the money, so treasurers should sign the checks." And, yet, it's exactly *because* they are in charge of the books and presenting the information to the board that treasurers shouldn't be able to sign checks.

A board president should be the first choice to be a check signer. After all, the executive director ideally will be meeting with the board president anyway. And signing checks can be a good way for a board president to better understand the business of the organization.

### How not to become essential

You probably have met board volunteers—often with the title of board president—who by sheer force of will carry an organization forward and reach new heights the nonprofit wouldn't have otherwise.

A nonprofit won't last long without passionate people who are willing to pitch in when needed. But you should *not* be the only one doing the work. The danger of taking too much on yourself is that everyone else will let you do it. And when it comes time for your term to end, guess what? No one wants your job! Because they all think they have to do everything you did.

If you want to serve as board president for a year, maybe two, you need to make sure that you haven't made the job look so unpalatable that no one wants it when you're done. Spread the work around! If you're feeling overwhelmed, email some of your key board members (other executive committee members or committee chairs) and ask them to manage a task.

Let board members step up without asking. Give them time and space to identify a problem themselves before you jump in to fix it. Maybe more tasks *would* get done if you did everything yourself. But not everyone is a superhero like you. You will find getting everyone working together is more effective over the long run than taking it all on yourself. Especially when it's time to step down.

Also, and this is especially important, *don't* ask for the board's sympathy or drop hints about how hard you're working. It's often ingrained in us at work to toot our own horns about the extra hours we put in, but here it can backfire. "I can't even guess how many hours I spent on this, or long nights on the phone I had talking about this, but now that this new strategic plan is done, I think the hard work has really paid off."

Thanks for putting in the time! But no one else is going to want your position if it means countless long nights on the phone. You just made it harder for yourself to step down. Be conscious about how you communicate about your own work to the board.

## Find your replacement

It's not out of line for a board president to take another board member out for coffee and suggest the person consider standing for nomination to be the next board president. In fact, something like this generally *should* happen. The governance or nominations committee can lead the process of identifying possible good candidates, but at some point someone is going to have to sit down and ask another board member to consider it.

The best someone to do that is probably you. Why? Because

the sitting board president can answer better than anyone else what the job requires. It's easy for a board member who has never served as a board president to nominate someone else for the job. But the sitting board president is going to be able to present a stronger case to the potential nominee.

You still want to have an open call for nominations. If multiple board members are nominated (or nominate themselves), you can conduct your election with a secret ballot vote. But most likely, you'll be faced with the problem of finding a candidate rather than having too many. A board president who works in advance to find a good candidate will not feel pressure to "stay on one more year" because no one else is stepping up.

## Using the soft power of board leadership

Being board chair doesn't mean you get your way all the time. Let's say you want to be board president because you want to push your organization in a particular direction. If you start pushing too hard, you're going to find that either one of two things happen. One—you get immediate resistance from board members and staff. Or two—you encounter not resistance exactly, but quiet. No one wants to stand up to argue because they can't match the strength with which you're pushing. So they stay quiet, stop coming to meetings, and maybe just slip away.

Neither are good outcomes.

You will get your organization a lot further in the direction you want to go if you adjust both your expectations and your methods.

Instead of looking at achieving your goal as one big Herculean effort, a successful board president will probably find that their legacy is in several thousand fingerprints that, combined, nudged the nonprofit forward. The tone you set at meetings; the culture and policies you leave behind; the way you treat members who disagree with you; how you approach conflict; how well you listen; the style with which you lead a meeting... Getting those things right will have a bigger impact on the direction the nonprofit goes than almost anything else you do.

From my own experience, I can share a short anecdote here. When I became president of the board of Tacoma360, I didn't know that during that year we would end up merging with another nonprofit come December. I didn't come to the job with any strong personal priorities, which was good. Because if I'd had them, I would have had to let them go very quickly. The alternative would have been wasting time fighting against the direction we *needed* to be going because I had a particular idea in mind of what my "legacy" should be.

The legacy I left was in the successful merger (with grant funding transferred over).

But let's not get too fixated on this idea of "legacy."

Not everyone gets to have one. The great presidents of the United States—Washington, Lincoln, Roosevelt—got to leave immense legacies. But did Millard Fillmore? Did Benjamin Harrison?

Often, keeping the ship from falling off course during your watch is legacy enough.

# EIGHT

# A LEADERSHIP POSITION FOR DENNIS

AFTER TWO YEARS of serving on the fundraising committee, the outgoing president called up Dennis and invited him
out for coffee.

"Dennis, the governance committee asked me to talk to you
about a possible leadership position on the board. You've really
dug into fundraising since you've started and—I have to tell you
—it hasn't gone unnoticed. Our fundraising is up, and everyone
credits that to your great job getting the board motivated—and
making it fun, too. The committee was wondering whether you
have thought about stepping up and using that same skill as vice
president, and maybe eventually as president."

Dennis was struck mute. He'd never considered such a position, and the fact that others, including the board president,
thought he was up to it, was flattering beyond measure. And
yet... he was fairly sure it wasn't for him.

"I'm honored that you would think of me. But I just don't
know if that's the right fit for me," he finally got out.

"I think you would be surprised," the board president said.
"The board has a lot of respect for you for all the ways you've

contributed in the last two years. I'd be happy to tell you more about the job if you're worried about the duties or the workload."

"I really am honored, but..." and Dennis took a deep breath, "I've been thinking about something a little different these last few months. I've really enjoyed helping with fundraising but it's also got me interested in something else. I know Bob is term-limited off the board this year, so he won't be treasurer ... I don't know if I have enough experience, but I'd work my butt off so that I got up speed. I just think—"

The board president cut Dennis off with a laugh. "Dennis, you don't have to be so nervous! Are you saying you'd rather be treasurer than vice president?"

Dennis nodded. It was hard to advocate for himself, especially since he still felt like such a newbie to the board process, but he got up the courage to say, "I do. I think I'd be a really good treasurer."

The board president smiled and nodded. "You know what? I think you would, too."

NINE

# CONCLUSION

SERVING on a board is a rewarding experience that will stretch your mental muscles and introduce you to new people you might not have met otherwise. It is enriching and a great way to give back to your community.

But that doesn't mean it is easy. My hope is that this book, or whatever piece of it that was most relevant to you, will help you get a lay of the land about your duties and the expectations you should have for yourself and your fellow board members.

When a professional theater in my hometown of Tacoma closed its doors about ten years ago, one of the board members was quoted in the local paper. She said, "I thought we got to help pick the plays."

As someone who loves theater and wants it to flourish, it was a punch to the gut to think that a board member at a struggling theater company would say that. It's *not* her fault she thought she got to pick the plays. It's a failing of the entire board, who never properly educated her (and likely, several other members) about what it *really* means to be a board member and the important responsibilities of a board.

The seeds for this book—and my hope of helping board members of small nonprofits all over the country—were planted when I read that quote. I sincerely hope that this has been helpful to you, and maybe for your whole board. I hope your board is able to lead the way for years to come, and make the change in your community or in your world that you want to see. My hat is off to you—you are doing some of the most important work there is.

Thank you.

# PART THREE

# APPENDICES

# TEN

# APPENDIX A - ROBERT'S RULES OF ORDER

*ROBERT'S RULES of Order* is the standard manual used during a "parliamentary" meeting such as a board meeting. It is designed so that in every possible contingency you can think of, there's a prescribed way to handle it. Some nonprofit bylaws call out *Robert's Rules of Order* as the basis for running meetings.

The book was first published in 1876 by Henry Martyn Robert, a U.S. Army Colonel. And at times... well, you can tell it's based on the ideas of a nineteenth-century military man.

The entire set of rules is laboriously complex. As an elected official who sits on a legislative body that uses *Robert's Rules*, I have read a lot (but not all) of the book. And I can tell you, without a doubt, it's boring. I have met only one or two nonprofit board members who have picked up a copy.

There is, thankfully, a "brief" version. It's still two hundred pages, but that's a lot shorter than the long one. Your nonprofit may wish to buy a copy of the short version and have it at the meeting, just to have around on the off chance you need it.

Despite how few people have read the book, *Robert's Rules*

*of Order* is the standard basis for running meetings. If you've served on almost any board, you likely are familiar with the gist of it.

What is the point of this old-fashioned system? At its most basic, it prevents meetings of groups of people (including unions, political parties, clubs, and associations) from descending into chaos. It also provides a structural way to give a dissident a path to make their case or, at least, go on record as being against a particular measure.

Here is an overview of how votes are taken under *Robert's Rules of Order*, especially as they are frequently used by small nonprofits:

———

First, someone makes a "motion." A board member could say, "I move to adopt the budget as presented." The next step: Someone "seconds" the motion. This is what allows the board to consider something for a vote. (The board secretary should record the names of the originator of the motion and the second.)

If no one chooses to second the motion (which is unlikely but possible), it's dropped and nothing happens.

At this point the board discusses the motion. No other business of the board can happen until the motion has been resolved. (In *Robert's Rules of Order*–speak, the motion is considered "privileged.")

How is a motion resolved? Generally by a vote.

After discussion, the board president will say, "Seeing no other questions or comments... all those in favor of the motion, please signify by saying 'Aye.'" Then everyone in favor votes. "All opposed, please signify by saying 'Nay.'" Then everyone against the motion votes. (The board secretary records the results.)

Sometimes a board president will say at this point, "Abstentions?" Someone who has a conflict of interest might voice their name here. Unless you have a specific reason for abstaining, you should vote for or against the motion and not sit it out. Even if you don't like either option, voting is part of your job.

In a small board meeting, this kind of voice vote is usually enough for the president and the secretary to tell whether a vote has passed, and who voted on which side. But sometimes it's not clear. If either the president or the secretary is unsure, they should ask for a roll-call vote in which everyone gives their vote one at a time so there is no confusion.

The two results of the vote are simple to understand: a motion can be approved (the majority vote for it), or it can be defeated (the majority vote against it).

Sometimes, though, a motion can be resolved without a vote if the board votes to "table" it, which means the board instead votes to postpone further consideration of the motion until a later meeting.

*Robert's Rules of Order* have something like 15 pages on how to "table" a motion, and there is specificity about whether it's coming back at another or just being removed indefinitely. Almost no nonprofit I've seen uses this. Simply "tabling" a motion (often without a vote as in the example above) is a norm.

In fact, most nonprofits fudge on *Robert's Rules* in a variety of ways. For example, almost all nonprofits will discuss a topic for a while before anyone actually makes a motion on it, as opposed to making the motion and then discussing it.

You might also find these concepts useful to working with *Robert's Rules of Order*:

.  .  .

*"Point of Information."*

A motion is on the table. You can always ask for clarification on what is at stake and what a "yes" or a "no" vote means. If you want to do that, you say "Point of Information" and then ask your question. You may not actually need to say it in a regular meeting, but if things are contentious and you are legitimately asking for information (and not arguing), you may want to preface your question.

*"Call for the question."*

If a debate is going on and on and on, you can "call for the question." This forces the board to decide whether to continue debating. If two-thirds of the board votes that they are ready to vote (on the motion at hand), the voting takes place immediately. In practice, though, by the time *you're* exhausted from debate, so are most other board members. If you call for the question, a board will often just get on with the vote on the motion.

*"Friendly amendments."*

There's no such term in *Robert's Rules of Orders*, but again: it's common at board meetings of small nonprofits. Basically it means that someone in favor of the motion suggests something that would improve the original motion, or make it more palatable to someone who is not currently in support. For example: "I'd like to suggest a friendly amendment, Bob. Where it says, 'term limits are three years long,' I'd like to suggest we add the phrase 'renewable once.'" For some reason this is directed to Bob (the person who made the original motion in my example), and Bob can choose to accept it, or not. This is workable shorthand for amending a motion. If there have been any amendments (friendly or otherwise) to a motion, the board president should always reaffirm the final text of the motion being voted upon before calling for the vote.

Those are the most common ways that *Robert's Rules of Order* are used during a small nonprofit board meeting. Again, it's a good idea for a board to have a single copy of the rules (or the brief version) handy at meetings in case something more complex comes up.

(This chapter is also available as a printable "cheat sheet" at http://forsmallnonprofits.com/boarddocs.)

# ELEVEN

# APPENDIX B - HOW TO UPDATE YOUR BYLAWS

BYLAWS ARE OFTEN several pages long, and densely packed with minutiae about elections, terms, and more. They're daunting to tackle, but going through an official process to review and revise them holds the key to the majority of real reform opportunities for your board. Let's cover the basics of bylaws and then look at the ways your nonprofit might consider changing them.

### What are bylaws for?

Bylaws are the most basic rules of operation for your board and nonprofit. They should cover only the highest level of operation of the board. Think of the bylaws as equivalent to the U.S. Constitution—broad in the topics it covers and infrequently changed—while the policies you pass are more like the laws that fit within its framework. Every time Congress passes a law, it doesn't have to amend the constitution. Keep your bylaws focused on the big picture and use policy to enact other changes.

Here are the common things you'll see in a set of bylaws: the mission or goal of the organization; definition of membership (if applicable); the rules for notification of meetings where business is transacted; the basics of the board (size, terms, how to remove board members, size of quorum, etc.); designation of officers and their duties; elections of board members and officers; standing committees and their goals; term of the fiscal year; and process for amending the bylaws.

What follows are things to look for as you review your bylaws.

## Look for the easy changes first

A lot of what you read in your nonprofit bylaws is probably fine. Look for "housekeeping"-style changes, which just clean up the document to make it match current conditions: updating your address, adding that email (not just regular mail) is appropriate for notice of meetings, or changing the list of standing committees to reflect that your board development committee is now called a governance committee. These will be noncontroversial changes for the rest of the board.

## Remove overly specific language

If you try to overly prescribe the business of your nonprofit in the bylaws, you will find yourself in bylaw paradoxes or otherwise needing to change your bylaws all the time.

Let me give you an example of an overly prescribed set of bylaws that went terribly wrong. A board I worked for proposed a change that said that the president of the board should be president-elect of the board for a year before assuming the duties. Makes sense, right? You can learn the job before you get to it, and it sets up a clear leadership succession plan.

Elsewhere in the bylaws, though, was a rule that any officer of the board had to have served on the board for a year. This also makes a certain amount of sense, as it would ensure that the board has leadership that understands the board culture and the organization.

But together these rules went badly wrong. First, when the president-elect stepped down partway through her term, there was a real succession problem: whoever would be president for the next year would, by default, not have served as president-elect *for a year*. Which meant that, technically, the board didn't have anyone eligible to be president anymore.

In addition, the board had added two or three really great people mid-year, but none of those people had served on the board for a full year, and so were ineligible to be an officer, such as president-elect. Other board members were term-limited off the board that year and couldn't stand for another term. Between the various bylaws rules, on a board of thirteen there were fewer than three people who were even eligible to be president-elect, and that didn't solve the issue that no one was technically eligible to be president at the start of the fiscal year (except the current president).

The board did what many boards do in scenarios like this: it ignored the bylaws and did its best, referring the bylaws back to the governance committee for fixing the issue as part of the committee's annual review. But if the issue had been contentious—let's say that someone didn't support the nominee for the next president—the bylaws would be unclear and confusing at the worst possible time.

The bylaws are most important when there is real disagreement, which is why removing language that might create one of these paradoxes is important.

So again, not everything has to be in the bylaws. It might be good to simply have the norm that presidents serve as president-elect first.

Also, remember that a board has another tool in its tool belt besides the bylaws: the ability to make policy. Just because it's not in the bylaws doesn't mean it's not important. The bylaws should be the broadest set of rules that allow a board to make decisions. They shouldn't be a list of all the policies of the board.

## Determine an ideal board size

What is the appropriate size of the board? It doesn't have to be in the bylaws, but whatever you think the ideal number is, the bylaws should provide a flexible range for you. If you want an ideal board of fifteen, for example, then allow your board a range of nine to seventeen. By allowing for a wide gap at the bottom between the ideal board and your bylaws-specified minimum, you are ensuring you aren't forced into taking someone on the board just to stay above the minimum. Having a maximum that is slightly bigger than your ideal board allows you to add that extra person you really want when they come along, and not be in violation of the bylaws because you're already full.

(Boards are often filled with an odd number of members, to prevent tie votes, although I've never seen a tie vote on a nonprofit board, or even a vote in which a single vote meant the difference. It's rare, but that's the reason you'll often see the ideal board size set at an odd number.)

## Establish terms

Does your board have terms? If not, this should be an easy decision to make. As discussed before, terms help a nonprofit know how long it can expect to have a board member's expertise on the board. Terms also enable board members to step down gracefully if they choose, by not standing for another term.

If you don't already have terms, I'd recommend establishing a three-year term. Shorter than that, and a board member is practically done with their term as soon as they start. Longer terms might dissuade people from joining the board.

For three-year terms, the terms themselves should be staggered so that the terms of roughly one-third of the board are up every year. That way the entire board isn't up for renewal in the same year. (This doesn't necessarily have to be in the bylaws, but it's useful to know.)

Adding terms just formalizes the relationship a bit. This change shouldn't be controversial...

### Consider term limits

... But this one probably will be. There are some really good reasons to consider term limits.

*Term limits help a board stay current with changing times.*

What worked ten years ago might not work now, but it often takes new people with new ideas to realize that.

*Term limits help prevent an individual board member from accumulating too much power over the rest of the board.*

As a new board member, it's hard to argue with someone who's been there for twenty years. Board members who have been there that long will just get their way because no one wants to argue with them.

. . .

*Term limits allow a board to grow in experience, vision, and financial capacity—especially the board of a small nonprofit.*

What started out as a group of engaged volunteers with a dream could grow to become a community institution with stable resources and a big impact. But it's hard to get there with just the original group of volunteers.

*Term limits help prevent board members from getting tired.*

Even on committees or boards I've loved, I've often been quietly relieved to term out and step down. What you personally get out of an organization as a volunteer board member can slowly start to decrease over time. Eventually board business might all start to feel like stuff you've been through before. Maybe you became a little cynical, maybe the excitement is gone, and you feel that you're just looking over budgets all the time. Term limits help prevent burnout.

*Term limits remove board member guilt.*

Board members don't have to feel bad about being burned out or about wanting to move on. They can end their time gracefully.

Here is one example of how you add term limits to your bylaws. After spelling out the terms for board members, the bylaws could say:

*These terms are renewable, but no person shall serve more than two (2) consecutive full terms.*

And that's it! It's such a small change to the bylaws... and yet it's often a massive hurdle to implement. The problem is that the organizations that need term limits the most are the least likely to adopt them.

Sometimes people like to stay for years and years on a

board. Maybe they founded the organization and believe they are irreplaceable (or believe that they are protecting the organization's roots from people who want to go in a new and scary direction). Maybe they have a profound sense of self-identity tied up with their position on the board. Maybe they are a major donor and believe that they are entitled to a position on the board. Maybe they simply love the organization and want to stay as close to it as possible.

Whatever the reason, even bringing it up can create bitter feelings in those who would be forced to term off the board. Here are some ideas that might make that transition a little easier.

*Create an emeritus board or an advisory council.*

This option might be a good one for nonprofits that want to keep good donors close to the organization. They create a much larger council of the best donors, previous board members, founders, and more, and use them as a sounding board for important issues.

For example, I sat for a four-year term on the alumni council of my college. We met twice a year and had some responsibilities—you don't want to create a group that *truly* does nothing—but we didn't have the legal and fiscal oversight of the college. Your nonprofit could consider something similar. Board members who are termed out might be happy sitting on a group like that.

*Deem every current board member to be in their first term.*

While I was the director at the Grand Cinema, the board implemented term limits, but used this caveat: everyone was considered to be in their first term. This put all board members onto a level playing field. People who might have been termed off the board in one year instead had four years remaining on the board, or more.

If I recall correctly, this passed unanimously, even by people who had been on the board for many years. If this compromise makes it possible for your board to implement term limits, it's a good solution.

You can either draw straws to get a staggered board rotation started after doing this, or ask for preferences and then sort it out as a committee.

*Hire an outsider.*

There are a variety of consultants who can help lead a board on issues like fundraising, governance, capital campaigns, strategic planning and more. They can be useful for addressing topics that might be painful for some to discuss—like term limits.

If the newest member to a board brings up term limits, the longer-serving board members may feel that they are being edged out. But a professional consultant who opens a discussion about term limits by framing it as "good governance" will likely get a better hearing, without seeming personally motivated.

After that initial facilitated discussion, it should be easier for a board or a governance committee to address the issue.

*Can board members come back?*

Let's say a board member served two consecutive terms, took three years off, and now wants to come back onto a board. Should you bylaws restrict that?

As I said before, this is the kind of thing you may not need to codify into the bylaws. Your board might have the norm of not bringing back old members. But a future board might have a good reason to, and you don't need to unnecessarily restrict that board from doing so.

*When shouldn't you have term limits?*

Are there any examples of small (or very small) nonprofits that shouldn't have term limits?

Yes. Sometimes very small nonprofits are just a group of volunteers who are trying to make a difference. When they've filled the need, or when the group dissolves, the work of the nonprofit dissolves. There's nothing wrong with that. A lot of the recommendations of policy may not apply to them, including the decision to institute term limits.

But if that group of volunteers wants the nonprofit to last past the group's own direct volunteer work, then all of these are important, including term limits. It's through these policies that the nonprofit can endure, even after the founding volunteers are ready to move on to something else.

Here's another example of when term limits might not be worth the fight: when dealing with a very generous board member. Some nonprofits have a single donor whose capacity for giving dwarfs that of the other board members so much that, without this donor, the nonprofit might cease to function. Such donors *should* give without having to be on the board, and they *should* recognize that by operating this way they are holding back the organization over the long term. But they may not. And that's an awfully hard person to imagine approaching about this idea.

This nonprofit should have term limits, since it very much needs to diversify the funding streams and the number of people who care about it. But I wouldn't blame a board member who decided not to pick this battle at this time.

## Nominations and elections

As we continue to look through the bylaws for possible changes, one thing to look at is the question of how board members are elected to the board.

Generally, the board appoints new members to fill the seat on the board for a particular term. It's a vote of the board members themselves. There's no reason to change this model if that's what you have in place.

Some nonprofits, though, are membership organizations that have a body of members outside the board who elect board members to represent them. Both of the nonprofits I led as the director had this structure and I watched both boards struggle with the same question: "Should we have *real* elections?"—real, meaning that someone would win, and someone would lose for each available seat on the board.

After seeing both nonprofits implement this for at least one round of nominations, I have to say I don't recommend it. First, it makes recruiting new members slightly more challenging, since someone has to stand for election, yet might not get on the board. Second, when a board member steps down from a board mid-term, the people who lost are frequently called upon to fill that vacant seat—so, what was the point of a competitive election? And third, I've twice seen sitting board members fail to be elected back to a board for a second term.

Of course, this might be the exact argument for why a board should have competitive elections. But from what I saw, it was a real blow to those—now former—board members. It's impossible to not take that personally. Giving is likely to suffer, and it's awkward to thank and recognize those departing board members for their service.

If you have three seats to fill on a board, I'd recommend the board put forward three candidates to the membership to fill it.

Finally, some nonprofits' bylaws allow for other means of getting onto a board. For example, the chair of a certain important committee might automatically become a board member or another agency or nonprofit might have an automatic seat on your board of directors. If your nonprofit has these backdoor ways to get onto a board, I'd look to close them. Let your norms handle this instead. All board members should enter through the same gate.

## Voting to remove a board member

Your board may have the ability to remove a board member from a seat by a majority vote. It rarely happens, but a board member who just stops showing up and doesn't reply to email would need to be removed in this manner.

Here's one way to phrase it in your bylaws: *Any Director may be removed at any time from the Board for cause by a majority of the Board.*

Here's another: *A Director may be removed from office by a two-thirds majority vote at a regularly scheduled board meeting where the item was placed on the written agenda distributed at least one week ahead.*

I'm including both of these options because although they are superficially the same, I think one is better than the other, and I want to contrast them to make a larger point.

So which one is better?

The first that allows just a "majority?" Or the second in which a "two-thirds" majority is needed? Does that make a difference?

Here's a hint: it has nothing to do with how big the majority is.

The second one is better because it doesn't include the phrase "for cause." Removing the phrase "for cause" allows the board to decide whether it wants to act or not, without having to spend time deliberating on whether there is "cause."

Yes, *of course*, you don't want a board to willy-nilly remove board members from office without cause. But if it's even come up, then there *is* cause (at least some board members think so). Removing the phrase allows the board to focus on the specifics of the situation and not whether the current situation "counts." And I promise—if this is a matter of debate, at least one board member will ask if this qualifies as appropriate cause.

The larger point here is this: the bylaws should set the ground rules of allowable actions. They are like a big "Frequently Asked Questions." Someone asks the bylaws, "Can a board remove a board member from office?" And the bylaws answer: "Yes, with a two-thirds majority vote." They shouldn't wade too far past that level. Following bylaws in a difficult situation is hard enough without having to try to divine what the original authors meant when they wrote something like "for cause."

## Recalls

If you have a membership-based organization, it *might* be possible that the members have the power to call a meeting and throw out board members (or the whole board). It's easy to look at this and think: "Eh. Probably won't happen." And it probably won't.

*But don't even give them a chance.* A board has a legal and fiscal responsibility to the organization that ordinary members don't have. A board that carefully and deliberately votes to cut a beloved program that is bleeding money should not be looking over its shoulder and wondering if there will be a recall by the members in two weeks to throw them out because of it.

For the most part, recalls are an issue only in organizations in which members can vote for the board. But the option to recall gives the general membership too much power. If the membership doesn't like a course of action, then it's at the next election when it should get to vote for a preferred candidate —*not* in between elections in the heat of the moment.

Get rid of this.

### Voting by email and voting by proxy

With the advent of technology, it's often tempting to want to get more done by email or conference call.

In general, I would recommend that your bylaws allow for votes over email (at times when *everyone* is voting by email), or votes via a conference call.

In my home state there are laws about email voting for boards and how it works. Your state may have similar statutes. It's worth a check with a nonprofit attorney before you enact email voting.

Even if legal, email voting should be used sparingly, though. Discussion that would have happened in person often won't happen via conference call, and email threads can often get extremely difficult to follow. Your board should have the expectation and the norm that people attend.

Voting by proxy, on the other hand, should be done away with. Let's say a vote is coming up on authorizing a new program estimated to cost $25,000. A board member who will be absent writes, in advance, a "yes" vote and gives it to a board member who will attend the meeting (that person attending the meeting is considered to "be a proxy" or "have a proxy vote" for the person who couldn't attend). But then at the meeting, the executive director says that new information has come to light that indicates the program will actually cost $50,000. How should the proxy vote be treated? Is it a "yes vote" because the board member who gave the proxy vote wanted the program? Or a "no" because the program is too expensive? It's impossible to say without asking—but of course, you can't. Otherwise, there's wouldn't be a need for the proxy.

Voting by proxy is fundamentally different from email or a conference call, when all board members are privy to the same information, because of the chance of new information arising after the vote has been made. Dump it.

### Email notifications are fine

That said, boards often require a certain number of days of notice before an official meeting. That's fine, but make sure that notice can be delivered by email. Some bylaws still call for mail, and in this day and age with rising postage costs and the convenience of email, there's just no reason for that.

### Number of meetings

If your bylaws call for a mandatory minimum number of board meetings per year, and that number is larger than ten, you may want to decrease it. Even six or eight might be safer. Again, you can meet monthly (and probably should) but what if your board often doesn't meet in December because it's too hard to schedule people, and then a freak snowstorm prevents a meeting in February and in August too many people are on vacation and you can't get a quorum. Suddenly you're in violation of your bylaws. It's better to establish a lower number of meetings.

Quorums

Your board likely has a minimum number of attendees to be able to conduct official business. This is a good thing. It protects the organization from the whims of a small minority who happened to attend. It can be a frustration, though, if a board continually has trouble making a quorum.

Half of your current board members make for a good quorum. Avoid having two-thirds needed, and make sure that it's phrased as a percentage of current board members, not a flat number that assumes you have a full board.

But if your board is having trouble making a quorum, then your board needs to deal with that attendance issue outside of the bylaws. Adjusting the quorum shouldn't be your solution.

### Can an executive committee act on behalf of the board?

It might be a good idea to have an executive committee (usually composed of the officers of the board) who can act on behalf of the board in times of emergency or between board meetings. I would suggest you don't need to write into the bylaws that their actions need to be formally ratified by the board at the next meeting. Rather, if it's an unpopular decision, the full board can simply overturn it, or elect new leadership. (All of these scenarios are unlikely, but giving the board the duty to ratify makes it more likely they *won't*. Forcing the board to choose to overturn something is better than giving them the automatic option to do so.)

### Creating a committee structure

Your bylaws can spell out the essential committees of the board, the length of time someone can be chair, and a lot more. Sometimes that might be necessary based on your norms. But you can also allow real freedom by replacing it all with a simple sentence:

*The Board may designate committees: standing, ad hoc, or otherwise as it deems necessary.*

Maybe a marketing committee made sense in 2009. But if you don't need it now, your bylaws don't need to call for it. And, of course, the corollary to that is: Even if you *do* need it now, your bylaws don't need to call for it.

# TWELVE

# APPENDIX C - CREATING AN EFFECTIVE COMMITTEE STRUCTURE

A BOARD'S committee structure will likely have a few standing committees and a few ad-hoc committees, depending on the size of the board and the needs of the organization. This appendix provides a summary of the most common committees, followed by ideas about scheduling, the number of committees you need, non-board members serving on committees, committee term limits, and more.

What are committees for?

*Committees should be where the work of the board happens.*

And board meetings are the place where that work is adopted as policy. A board of thirteen people shouldn't spend half of its meeting debating the finer points of a new policy. That work should happen in a committee before it gets to the board.

Here's an example: the governance committee brings a controversial proposed policy to the board, like term limits. The board talks about it for ten minutes, and the committee chair takes a lot of notes, answers questions, and invites continued feedback. Then the governance committee takes it back again and refines the proposal at its next committee meeting before coming back to the board with a revised draft. Maybe after another ten minutes, the same thing happens and it's referred back again. But at the next board meeting, it's ready for a vote.

This kind of back and forth between a committee and a board is essential to keeping the board focused on the big picture. Without a committee structure, this would involve the board arguing about the controversial proposal for long stretches of time, when the board should be focused on a range of issues and responsibilities.

*A good committee structure can also help remove the "personal" element that can come up around controversial policies.*

Members of the governance committee can advocate on behalf of a certain policy to the whole board without automatically being treated with suspicion. A loose group of board members who bring exactly the same policy forward might be viewed more skeptically—as if they have ulterior motives. They wouldn't have the formalized role of serving on a committee that helps clarify their responsibility or interest. It's a subtle distinction, but it's important.

*Committees help board members take ownership of key responsibilities and make sure the rest of the board is doing its due diligence.*

Without committees, it's too easy for bylaws or finances to not get the scrutiny they need.

Appendix C lays out the responsibilities of a variety of

committees your board may have and answers a lot more questions about how a good board structure should work.

What follows are the essential committees for a board to do its due diligence.

## Essential standing committees

### Finance committee

The treasurer of the nonprofit sits on the finance committee along with a group of people who conduct a "deep dive" into the finances of the organization. At a typical finance committee meeting, the executive director will present the monthly financial reports (usually a profit and loss statement and a balance sheet). There will be a discussion that compares the finances to the budget, or to the previous year. The executive director should flag anomalies and explain them, and answer questions from the committee.

There shouldn't be a lot of "judgment" in this committee meeting. The numbers are the numbers, no matter whether they are good or bad.

After the finance report, the committee could look at one of several bigger pieces of business. These might include reviewing reserves, hiring an audit firm, planning for next year's budget, or considering a major initiative that will require detailed financial models from the committee. Usually there's enough to keep this group very busy.

### Governance committee

As noted before, a governance committee is often called a board development committee. Whichever the name, the committee has a role to improve the individual skills of board members and to improve the processes of the board.

The first task, if it hasn't already been done, is a review of the bylaws and recommendations for change. That can keep this committee busy for months. If that's already done, the bylaws should be revisited only once a year, and if the big review has been done recently, the bylaws may not need to be changed the next time through. Maybe some tweaks are needed to remove confusing language, but by and large, once the bylaws have been through a recent revision, they shouldn't take up a lot of the committee's time.

The other responsibilities of the committee might include proposing changes to improve board meetings, planning a board retreat, identifying skill gaps on the board that need to be filled by new board members, nominating new board members or board officers, and recommending policy not specifically covered in the bylaws.

*Executive committee*

An Executive committee is the only "standing" committee listed here that might not actually have a standing meeting. This committee is usually composed of the key officers: president, vice president (or president-elect), treasurer, and secretary. Sometimes a board chooses to include the past president on this list as well.

The bylaws often allow for this committee to act on behalf of the board in an emergency or between board meetings. Because of that, it's often the executive committee that will meet if there is a sudden issue. Maybe the executive director needs an immediate approval of $5,000 to fix a safety concern; maybe the treasurer discovered a pressing financial matter; maybe two board members are having a strong dispute and it's affecting the business of the board.

As an executive director, I asked for an executive committee meeting for a variety of business, including giving advance notice to the group that I would be firing an employee. (While the board generally doesn't get to weigh in on these matters, in small nonprofits I found it to be useful to get buy-in from the board leadership first.)

Even though the executive committee may be called to meet based on immediate need, it's not a bad idea for the committee to have a standing quarterly meeting. This might enable it to catch board issues early, set the agenda for the next several board meetings, or use the time to give performance feedback to the executive director.

### Other potential standing committees

In addition to those three, the other common standing committees are fundraising (or membership), program, and marketing. These committees may straddle a line between the policy-making role of a board and the "implementing the policy" role of an executive director. "Good governance" suggests that straddling the line in this way is probably not a good idea. That said, these committees wouldn't be so common at small nonprofits if there weren't ways they could be helpful.

I'd say the most common risk of these committees is creating needless work for the executive director. It's important that the board president or committee chair remind committee members of their committee's specific role and the best way to fulfill that role.

Here's a short snapshot of these committees and how they can work best.

*Fundraising or membership*
Fundraising is a key responsibility of the entire board. It's

usually a key duty of the executive director, as well. A fundraising committee can help make sure that everyone is on the same page.

The role of the fundraising committee is to coordinate the fundraising work of the full board. The committee members are *not* the primary fundraisers. A board needs to fully understand this before it creates this committee. This committee might make connections with donors or foundations, it might strategically look at the annual event and consider new options, it might recommend a target budget for the next fiscal year. The committee might also do more mundane work, like making thank-you calls or stuffing envelopes for one meeting straight. But I wouldn't let the mundane tasks become the sole purpose of the committee. That kind of work should be, at most, a way for them to chip in at crunch time.

(If your organization is membership-based, and membership revenue is a key revenue stream, then instead of a fundraising committee, you might have a membership committee that takes on similar tasks.)

*Marketing*

There is little "policy" work to be done on a marketing committee, and I wouldn't recommend it as a standing committee unless the executive director was new to marketing or the committee was hard to shut down for political reasons.

If this committee must exist, then it should focus on the high-level questions and broader issues. Who is the target market? What demographic information do we know? How can we collect it? What is our marketing plan? What should be on an annual marketing calendar?

All are good questions and are a much better use of time than a meeting that critiques a brochure design for 45 minutes.

If a member of the committee does have particular expertise in design or public relations, I recommend that the majority of "implementation" work be done outside of the committee meetings. If a new press release needs to be drafted, it doesn't need to happen at the meeting, with four members chiming in. Maybe the executive director and the PR expert send a draft back and forth via email once or twice before the meeting. Either way, going "big picture" uses the talents of the entire committee much more wisely.

*Program*

Program committees can mean many things depending on the organization, but generally a program committee is looking at the core function of the organization. At its best, a program committee could review data on participation rates, service effectiveness, survey results, reports to granting organizations, and other high-level reviews. The program committee of an arts organization might review audience feedback; at a homeless shelter it might interview current and former residents; at an environmental nonprofit, it might look at volunteer participation rates.

Working with the executive director, this committee could also look at national trends in the nonprofit's field. What new models in service delivery are emerging? What are the new trends in the expectations of foundations and grant-making organizations? What are the best practices that have been established in the field? Could the professional and personal connections of the committee or board be used to attract new partners for the organization?

That's a pretty ideal version of the program committee. The huge risk of having this committee is that it creates a band of four or five board members who may try to direct the executive director's day-to-day work. This can be deadly. The executive director can feel that she's being second-guessed at every turn, that she no longer has the confidence of the committee, that she no longer has the ability to make decisions about the operations of the organization.

A board should take care to educate members who serve on this committee about their role. Much like the finance committee, this group should look at the big picture, watch for warning signs of possible disaster, and review the data without judgment. With mutual trust between the executive director and the board, this can be a powerful committee if it avoids the pitfalls.

## Ad-hoc committees

Ad-hoc committees are committees that are called for a particular task and disband when that task is complete. What follows are some of the most common ad-hoc committees you will find at small nonprofits.

### *Audit committee*

This was mentioned earlier under board responsibilities, but there are good reasons for an ad-hoc committee, and not the finance committee, to manage the audit. An audit committee adds an extra layer of security, because it might help uncover a situation such as a nonprofit's treasurer who has been colluding with staff to embezzle or conceal funds. This is rare, of course, but it's one reason boards might choose to have a separate audit committee.

This committee likely needs three to four meetings: the first to plan the process; the second to review bids and approve a contract; the third to review the findings of the audit; and possibly a fourth to prepare for a presentation to the board or continue review of the audit findings.

*Event committee*

A fundraising gala or breakfast fundraiser may have an ad-hoc committee to manage the details of the event or to give extra support to the executive director or other staffer who may be running it. Either way, this is a common committee that usually doesn't need to have a standing time on the calendar all year.

This committee should meet shortly after the annual event to discuss how it went and celebrate its success. After that, it can take a few months off before starting up again five or six months before the event. The larger the event, the more this committee starts to resemble a standing committee and not a temporary ad-hoc committee.

*Nominations committee*

If the governance committee's plate is full, a separate nominations committee can handle the coordination of reviewing candidates for the board. Such a committee should be expected to lay out a plan for this before getting started. Here's an example of a rough calendar:

- January—Nominations committee lays out schedule for nominations. Committee asks board members who are eligible if they are returning for another term; committee identifies ideal number of new board members and skills for which the board would like to recruit.
- February—Open nominations. Ask board members

to submit names and bios. A call for nominations is placed in the email newsletter.

- March—Confirm interest with nominees and schedule interviews.
- April—Interview candidates, and review board responsibilities and expectations with them. Committee makes final recommendations.
- May—Elect candidates to the board for their term starting in July.
- June—Nominations committee hands off names to the governance committee for board orientation.
- July—The new board members start their term.

This timeline has a full six months of meetings for the nominations committee. Some small boards might be able to do it in four, but I wouldn't suggest attempting it much faster than that. It's because the process can be so time-consuming that this committee is often distinct from the governance committee.

Sometimes the nominations committee handles nominations for board officers, as well. It's not that the committee selects between two candidates for president, but it *can* help recruit for these positions, "accept" nominations for officers of the board, or manage the election process. These tasks can fall to the governance or executive committee as well. But it is important that a committee does it. It's not good to be less than a month before a new fiscal year and still be asking, "Does anyone want to be president next year?" The process should be managed, and potential leaders identified as early as possible.

*Search committee*

A nonprofit board looking to hire a new executive director might create a search committee that is different from the executive committee. Maybe someone on the board has human resources experience, maybe the executive committee has other tasks related to the transition, or maybe the executive committee wants more input. Whatever the reason, this is a common ad-hoc committee for many nonprofits that are hiring an executive director. The larger the size of the board, the more benefit you will have from a separate committee managing this process.

This committee probably needs five meetings. The first to plan the schedule; the second to create a job description; the third and fourth for interviews; the fifth meeting to pick a candidate and make a recommendation to the board.

*Strategic committee*

I served as the executive director for a nonprofit that chose to create a special ad-hoc committee with key members from the finance and membership committees to review the strategic direction of the organization and make a recommendation. I like this idea a lot. It acknowledges the expertise of the board and gives them real work to do. But since the two standing committees still have their regular work to do, calling this group as an ad-hoc committee is a great idea. If you have issues or questions that transcend a single committee, this might be a good way to handle it.

*Technology committee*

I put this on the list because it's a good example of the many kinds of ad-hoc committees that might be useful to your nonprofit—not because I think every nonprofit needs a technology committee. But if you have a need—like evaluating a technology purchase that could transform your organization, or ensuring that your computers aren't running Windows 95—

there might be a good reason for one or two meetings from a special committee.

I will note again that such a committee treads into the job responsibilities of an executive director. But if the director is willing, and legitimately could use the outside expertise, then this committee can be useful.

### One note about ad-hoc committees

Joining an event committee or an audit committee that meets only a handful of times should not satisfy the expectation for board members to serve on a committee. Board members should be expected to serve on a standing committee throughout the year. Joining an ad-hoc committee is something extra.

### Inviting non-board members to join committees

Some boards allow—and even strongly encourage—non-board members to serve on committees. There are several benefits.

Some people simply can't be on the board due to scheduling or some other conflict. So a committee is a great place for them to lend their time and expertise. A committee also harnesses the wisdom of people with specific knowledge or expertise (e.g., marketing professionals can sit on a marketing committee).

It's useful for board recruitment, too. Committees are a great training ground for the board. You can get a sense of how well someone works in a group, how well they listen, and their larger interest in the nonprofit. Strong committee members can be wooed to join the full board.

There are some possible downsides, though, to having non-board members on committees. The main issue is that non-board members on committees might start to resent the board. Let's say a certain proposal comes forward from a committee that doesn't fly with the full board. Committee members might feel upset, but this is even more of an issue with non-board members, because they weren't at the meeting and are hearing about the decision secondhand. (On the other hand, this could be motivation for them to join the board.)

The other issue that might arise is when a committee has too many non-board members and goes "rogue," setting off on a path that is in conflict with the board's stated goals. It's not common, but when it happens it's really a reflection of how poorly the board has managed the work of the committee rather than of the rogue committee members. With active and engaged board members on all committees, it's much less likely to occur.

*Should your committees have term limits?*

Very few small nonprofits, in my experience, need committee term limits since most committees are just extensions of the board. That said, if your nonprofit has a committee that you expect will have a significant number of non-board members on it, then term limits might help you stagger the committee's roster and manage the ebb and flow of members better. Term limits would be even more important to have if you have a committee with a lot of non-board members on it that has a direct impact on operations.

In general, committee term limits are most helpful when you want to provide the same kind of structure to a non-board member that you do to a board member: clear expectations and a clear end point that allows a committee member to step down gracefully.

As with board term limits, committee term limits are likely to cause hurt feelings when you first implement them. There might be even more hurt feelings than on a board, because committee members don't get a vote. Approach it cautiously and decide early on if there are compromises that could be made or other ways to more directly deal with an issue.

*When should committees meet?*

Standing committees likely already have a time and place they have been meeting. If a certain day and time has always worked, go ahead and stick with it. At the beginning of a new fiscal year, it's a good idea for the committee to schedule the rest of the year, especially if there are new members on the committee. "Third Thursday at 3:30" is good to get on the calendar early. If you want to take December off, you can plan for it then.

Also, pay attention to a committee's meeting time as it relates to the calendar of the nonprofit. The committee should meet at least two weeks before the monthly board meeting. That way, if there is work that needs to be done in advance of the board meeting, the committee has time to complete it without rushing to get material to the board in time. This is especially true if your board packet goes out a full week before the meeting.

*How many committees should your board have?*

I've listed five possible standing committees and six possible ad-hoc committees, with a door open for more. But is there a limit to how many committees a board should have?

Yes, absolutely.

Board members should be expected to sit on a single standing committee (not counting officers who sit on the executive committee as well as their regular committee assignment).

And most committees for small nonprofits have, in my experience, fewer than six members and often fewer than four.

So do the math—how big is your board? How many groups of four can you create?

A board of fifteen might comfortably be able to fill four standing committees, an executive committee, and two ad-hoc committees at any given time. I'd say that's the upper range of what I'd expect of a board. A board of nine might have no more than two or three standing committees, the executive committee, and no other committees.

When it comes to committees, less is more. Every committee report takes up extra time at the board meeting and slightly scatters the attention of the board.

I'd aim for no more than three standing committees and no more than one ad-hoc committee at a time. Your fellow board members and your executive director will thank you.

Here's an example of what the Smallville Historical Society's committee list looked like over several years:

- 2013: Finance, Executive
- 2014: Finance, Executive
- 2015: Finance, Executive, Marketing
- 2016: Finance, Executive, Marketing, Governance, "Building & Grounds" (a special committee dealing with evaluating the historic character and maintenance needs of the pioneer cabin)
- 2017: Finance, Executive, Marketing, Governance, "Building & Grounds"
- 2018: Finance, Executive, Governance, Strategic Committee (ad-hoc)
- 2019: Finance, Executive, Governance, Fundraising, Audit (ad-hoc)

- 2020: Finance, Executive, Governance, Fundraising

You can see transitions here as the board's committees change with its needs. At the beginning, the board pays attention to the finances and marketing, but not much more. It starts to get its act together in 2016 and adds two committees, one dealing with governance, the other with the central work of the nonprofit: preservation of the historic pioneer cabin.

By 2018, that "building and grounds" work has created an assessment that is handed over to the strategic committee, which takes that work and helps the board turn it into a strategic plan of some kind.

With the creation of a fundraising committee after that, one wonders—will there be a capital campaign in the future for the Historical Society? Maybe, maybe not. But for a nonprofit even thinking about going down that path, this is the kind of progression of a committee structure you would hope to see.

# THIRTEEN

# APPENDIX D - BOARD RECRUITING

AT SOME POINT, probably soon, your board will have to deal with finding new board members. Ideally, you will have a wealth of options, and can pull from your donor base, your volunteer group, your committee members, or prominent leaders in your community.

If you want that full roster of potential board members, though, you can't start two months before your next fiscal year. You must give this process time. What follows are the tasks your nominations or governance committee should start early in the fiscal year.

### First, evaluate your board's skills

A board should be more like a chess set than a checkers set. In a set of checkers, all pieces are equal and can do the same thing. In a chess set, though, each piece has a different function; some can move diagonally, others only forward and back. Some can jump other pieces; others are most effective dealing with the immediate squares around them. Together they form a formidable team, complementing one another's strengths and backing up one another's weaknesses.

What are the different skills your board has? Here are some questions to ask yourself, either individually or as a committee.

Do your board members have professional experience in:

- Your nonprofit's area of service?
- Law?
- Finance or accounting?
- Human Resources?
- Business?
- Marketing?
- Fundraising?
- Capital campaign experience? (if your board is considering moving down that path)

If your board is missing talent in one of these areas, then finding someone with those skills is a good place to start as you think about recruitment. In addition, if you are about to embark on a specific strategic push, then it might make sense to continue to build that strength. As an example, even if you already have someone with business experience, it still might make sense to add more people with similar skills if you are preparing a new retail operation.

### Next, evaluate your board's diversity

Your board should be made up of diverse people.

As I wrote earlier, boards need a strong diversity of opinion, otherwise they run the risk of falling into "group think," because there are no different viewpoints to counter their limited experience. A board with only college graduates will not be as smart as a board with college graduates *and* someone with a GED. Counterintuitive, no? But the diversity of experience makes a board smarter.

There are many kinds of diversity you might want to see on a board: gender, race, sexual orientation, class, education, religious beliefs, political views, and a lot more.

That said, a board with diversity in educational experience and political views, but that is still all-white or all-male has a problem. A significant one.

To be clear, the problem is *not* that this non-diverse board has an "image" problem, or anything as simple as that.

A board with gender and ethnic diversity is two things. First, it is more just. (I expect that statement is self-evident.) Second, it is better able to serve the public than a non-diverse board.

I want to unpack that statement before we keep going. So let's ask ourselves: Why do gender and racial diversity *in particular* make a board stronger?

It results from a long history of white male privilege, both legally and culturally, in the United States. Without a doubt, significant strides have been made. But that legacy remains hard to shake. To many women and minorities, that legacy expresses itself a hundred times a day in ways that make it clear that they are the "other." On the other hand, straight white males, myself included, are so insulated from this reality that we often have to deliberately go out of our way to see how pernicious racial and gender bias and discrimination truly are.

In other words, a board that is all-male, or all-white, or both, has a *massive* blind spot, and that blind spot is affecting how the nonprofit beneath it functions at its most basic level.

The issues of race and gender affect society in a variety of ways, some big, some small. When it comes to nonprofits, these issues affect the *kinds* of services nonprofits deliver and they affect *how* they are delivered. A board without diversity is more likely to be blind to ways that the nonprofit it governs is falling into these traps.

And thus... a theater announces a new season with only white male playwrights. An educational nonprofit pays women 30 percent less than their male counterparts. An environmental nonprofit never arranges a work party to clean the creek in the "bad part" of town. A civic group orders a new set of nametag frames—blue for men, and pink for women. A social services nonprofit discovers that even though the community it serves is 20 percent African-American, only 5 percent of the people it serves are.

(In this last example, a non-diverse board may not even think to ask about the racial demographics of the population it serves and compare it with the racial demographics of the community. A board with real diversity very likely will.)

Again, this is not just about image—although, yes, if a newspaper starts to cover any of the preceding examples it will likely be a damaging blow to those nonprofits. This is about *service*. Your nonprofit is here for *everyone*.

The public at large—as expressed in the special tax designation it has allowed your nonprofit to enjoy and in countless other ways—is counting on you to serve your community. *All of it*. A key step toward ensuring that you are doing so to demonstrate at the very top, where decisions are made, that your board reflects the diversity of your community.

*Are there any exceptions, when diversity on a board should not be a goal?*

No.

. . .

*Really?*

Yes.

A Catholic organization will likely have a board with many people who share a Catholic faith. But not all members will necessarily be Catholic, and *within* that group of Catholics, there should be gender and racial diversity. After all, there are more than one billion Catholics worldwide and 75 million in the Unites States—something tells me there is a lot of opportunity for diversity there.

A women's shelter may have a lot of women on the board, but let's not forget that the women the shelter serves are escaping domestic violence, sexual assault, or other abuses that are mostly perpetrated by men. Given that, shouldn't men who are willing to stand up against this abuse be part of the service to these women?

*All* organizations should reflect diversity. A diverse board will help all nonprofits better live up to their mission.

*A quick note on recruiting a more diverse board*

Non-diverse boards might find themselves in a catch-22. So they've decided to be more diverse—but where to start? You should know that a board that has determined they need to diversify might find it to be slow going at first. As I've said, the most likely candidates are committee members, members of the organization, donors, volunteers, and other partners. If you don't have a diverse board, you may also not have a diverse pool of potential candidates to pull from.

In addition, demonstrating a commitment to diversity is about more than just the racial or gender make-up of your board. A nonprofit that is working to grow its diversity at all levels—including programming, marketing, and operations—should be able to find diverse people to reflect that on the board. A nonprofit that is not making real changes, but still wants to find people of color or more women to serve on the board will more likely struggle to find candidates. *A person of color or a woman will easily be able to see that they are being recruited to be a "token" representative on the board.* If you are truly committed to diversity at all levels, your board and nonprofit will need to demonstrate that in your actions before you can expect to significantly increase the diversity of the board.

## Ask a board to self-identify

Hopefully the preceding section is understood. But there is still an important question: *how* do you evaluate the board's diversity?

The governance committee *should not* just sit down and assign different races to people. You can't assume that you can tell someone's race by looking. That's how you wind up accidentally labeling someone who identifies as "Pacific Islander" as "Native American." You don't know until you ask.

At a board meeting, the governance chair should pass around a questionnaire to every board member. This is an *optional* form, allowing board members to self-identify to whatever level they see fit. The governance chair should say plainly that the committee is gathering data on the board's diversity, and that it doesn't want to guess. If a board member wants to know how the data will be used, the answer is (likely) threefold: internally at the board level, for reports to grant-making organizations (foundations often ask for statistics on the diversity of the board, staff, or clientele served), and for the public through the annual report or possibly other means. The information on the questionnaire, therefore, shouldn't be considered confidential. Board members should answer only questions of their choosing. You may decide not to have names on the questionnaires as well, in case someone is uncertain about identifying as a certain sexual orientation or age. Either way is fine: the main issue is the makeup of the board as a whole, not the specific details of any one member.

The form should have a place for gender, race, and age. Since you're going through the trouble of making the form, though, you may also want to consider sexual orientation.

Have a place for respondents to mark their identified gender, and after "male" and "female," include an "other" with a place for someone to write in their own. (If you identify with your own perceived gender, and always have, this might feel odd to you. But it's important to people who don't identify with their perceived gender. You won't know how someone identifies until you ask.)

Have a place for respondents to mark their identified race. The census designations are useful choices here, but again, include an "other" with a blank.

Have a place for age, with categories split by decade, or by every twenty years (0 – 19, 20 – 39, 40 – 59, 60+).

Have a place for people to mark their sexual orientation (straight, gay, bisexual, asexual, and again—other).

This data should be collected and presented back to the board either during a retreat or at a later board meeting. Ideally, using publicly available census data or other free online information, you may want to present it against the demographics of your town or county. No immediate action needs to be taken necessarily, but creating an awareness of the issue is an important first step.

## Ask for help

If after reading this section you think that your board would have a hard time discussing this topic, please know there are many organizations and consultants who help boards discuss these issues in safe ways. An outside facilitator can help your board and nonprofit through this process.

## Check terms and term limits

The board president, executive director, and governance committee should know early—likely within the first month or two of the fiscal year—which board members are ineligible to stand for another term based on term limits (if you have them). This is the minimum number of new board members you will need to replace.

Next, you should know which board members are finishing out a term and are eligible to stand for another one. You don't have to know if they are planning to stand for their second term (they may not know it themselves yet). But if you add this number to the first, you will know the maximum number of new board members you will need to find.

If you've staggered your board terms correctly, this number shouldn't be more than a third of your board.

Of course, board members are not just interchangeable warm bodies. The board members leaving your board will be taking with them a certain set of skills, experience, and insight. The governance or nominations committee needs to review the assessments of board skills and have a serious and candid discussion about what skills the board is losing (or might lose), what skills it wants to replace, and what skills it would like to add to the board.

## Brainstorm potential new members

At least six months before the start of the next fiscal year, the governance committee should brainstorm potential new board members. Places to look are among volunteers, committee members, donors, business leaders, community leaders, past board members, leaders of partner organizations, and representatives of the people you serve.

Another way to brainstorm potential candidates it is to review this list of qualities I look for in board members, and think about who comes to mind. Do any particular skills or qualities make you think of someone in particular?

*Shared Vision*

- Familiarity with the nonprofit and its mission
- A record of philanthropic giving to the nonprofit

*Personal Traits*

- An ability to work in groups as a leader or as a follower
- Enough courage to stand up for an unpopular position in front of a group of peers
- A willingness to be a team player when needed
- A willingness to roll up one's sleeves and do work (when requested)
- A willingness to listen

*Experience and Connections*

- Previous board experience
- A particular skill needed by the board right now or in the near future
- Ability to read a financial report and understand financial projections
- The time to attend board meetings and committee meetings
- Comfort with email and email etiquette
- Good connections in the community or with the population served

## Commonly sought-after board members

In my experience, there are certain types of people whom boards—no matter what kind of nonprofit they run—want to recruit. Knowing these common traits might also help you in your brainstorm.

*Boards are often looking for people with a finance or legal background.*

Their services are often in high demand (lawyers) or they can open up doors (bankers), so they can be very hard to woo onto your board. If you have one of these professionals within your sphere, definitely think of them as candidates.

Again, they can be hard to get. (Maybe nonprofits try to take advantage of them too much and they are wary about accepting?) Don't automatically assume a banker will be your treasurer and don't expect a lot of free legal advice from a lawyer. They might want to be on your board *because* they want to do something that is different from their work. Give them the space for that.

*Boards often want members who are connected politically.*

This can be helpful—to have a city councilmember or an elected official in your corner when a state or city funding contract is up for review. Keep in mind, though, that sometimes elected officials can do more good *off* your board, where they don't have a conflict of interest supporting you. They may also be infrequent attendees. Sometimes *former* elected officials can get you the "access" you are looking for without those issues.

*Boards often want members who are wealthy.*

As people step down from your board and new people step up, ideally your board will get wealthier. This means more money in donations, and better connections with other wealthy donors. On the whole, you should be looking to increase your board's average giving with new members. Good donors should always be considered for the board.

When new candidates for the board are interviewed, you should feel OK telling them the average board gift and letting them know the board is looking to increase it. This sets expectations, but their reaction will also give you a hint of someone's possible capacity.

That said, this is a slow process. Don't spend your time strategizing about how to get a local "big name" multimillionaire onto your board. Focus on improving the board's annual average gift size every year. It's a lot more practical than a moon-shot attempt to get Bill Gates to join your board.

. . .

*Board recruiting is about relationships*

In *The Little Book of Gold: Fundraising for Small (and Very Small) Nonprofits*, I caution nonprofits leaders about trying to tell someone about their nonprofit while simultaneously asking for money for it. People won't give (or won't give much) to a nonprofit they are just now learning about.

The same is true of asking someone to be on a board. "Let me tell you about this nonprofit I love... Say, would you like to join the board?"

Prospective board members should have a relationship with the nonprofit to be good candidates for the board. You might hear a board member say, "My good friend Wayne is passionate about the issues we address every day, and he is great on boards. I know he's not familiar with what we do specifically, but I think he'd be a great board member." It is possible, if not likely, that Wayne *would* be a great board member. But instead of a cold invitation to join the board, it makes a lot more sense to invite him to attend the annual fundraising breakfast, to take a tour of the facilities, or to serve on a committee. Sometimes, a cold invitation will pay off. But generally you will do better to introduce someone early in the nominations process and then ask them to join later, even if it's just a few months later. This is one reason that having a nominations brainstorming session early in the fiscal year is a good idea—you have time to get people into your sphere.

## Inviting people to stand for nomination

At this point you should have an idea of how many seats you have to fill; the skills, experience, and diversity you'd like to add to the board; and maybe some possible names.

The governance or nominations committee should make a presentation to the full board about all of this. Early on, it should ask the board to be thinking about high-quality candidates to consider approaching. These candidates don't have to meet the exact profiles of the ideal board member that the committee has identified. But they should still be good fits.

Board members should use their relationships and ask their connections if they would "like to be nominated." Again, board members don't just get to invite someone to join the board and expect that it is a done deal. *There should be no expectation that everyone nominated will be accepted.* In fact, a nominations committee should look for at least twice the number of potential candidates to ensure a good pool of people to consider.

Board members should ask for a short bio from people who would like to stand for nomination, and give their contact information to the chair of the nominations committee. Candidates for the board should expect to have to provide information such as a resume or biography, possibly a questionnaire, and hopefully an in-person meeting with the nominations committee.

If someone balks—"Wayne just doesn't have the time for that. Do you really have to meet with him? Can't you just go by his reputation [or my recommendation]?"—then that should be a red flag. A candidate not willing to prepare a short bio or meet for thirty minutes to be interviewed is not going to be a very hard worker once on the board.

That said, I totally sympathize with candidates for a board who don't want to stand for a "real" election by a vote of the membership. A board that puts forward to its membership more names than it has seats for, knowing that some candidates will lose that election, is going to have a harder time during recruiting than a board that doesn't do this.

As early as possible in the process, candidates should also be given some documents. The most common would be the profit and loss statement and the balance sheet. Some nonprofits have a "memorandum of understanding" (described earlier in this book) for all board members, and that would be a good document to add. If it's as easy as attaching a PDF to an email, you might as well include a strategic plan, the bylaws, or the annual budget as well. None of this should be secret anyway, so feel free to share it with a candidate interested in the board. If you can distribute this information before candidate interviews, then when you meet them, pay attention to which candidates appear to have reviewed the material and which haven't.

Once the nominations committee has met with candidates, it should discuss the candidates and bring a preferred list of names to the board with a secondary list of names as well. This could be as simple as a ranked list, or it could be more specific— "If we can't get Mary, then we would want Dennis instead. If we can't get Lucy, then we would want Jamie."—based on the particular mix of skills and strengths the board is trying to create.

Some board members may want to know why the committee is recommending the slate of nominees over someone they nominated (and might be friends with). The committee should be honest about the decision-making process but focus more on the strengths of their candidates than on the weaknesses of those they aren't recommending.

After discussion, the names and their order should be approved in one vote, unless there is significant disagreement about a single candidate. This is one area in which the policy of something coming before the board one month, with a vote on it the next, probably shouldn't apply, though the spirit of it should. Ideally, a board will already be familiar with the names under consideration from the previous meeting. That meeting— not the one with the final slate of recommended candidates— would have been the time to object to one of the names or to advocate on someone's behalf.

Sometimes board members might have personal information they don't want to share in the group setting ("I worked on a board with Wayne and he was actually really hard to work with"). Board members should call the governance chair with these concerns as early as possible, and they should expect to be able to offer their opinion without it becoming public knowledge on the board. They should also be understanding if Wayne is one of the final candidates despite their personal misgivings.

All in all, if the nominations committee has kept the board informed throughout, there should not be any major surprises about the list of final candidates. The vote should be quick and easy.

To protect the feelings of the candidates not chosen, I recommend the committee begin its work quickly after the vote. Once approved, the governance committee should call and email the candidates the board has approved *the next day*. If someone wants to back out at this point, the committee will ideally have a backup name approved by the board. Those people should be contacted quickly as well. Only once the nominated candidates have been reached and agreed to serve on the board should the committee notify those who weren't selected.

Of course, no one likes being passed over. Candidates who weren't selected should be reminded that it's about more than just the individuals considered; it's about the mix of skills on the board. For good quality candidates that there just wasn't room for, the committee should encourage them to join a committee or otherwise further their relationship with the nonprofit.

## Orientation

After a new board member has been selected, I've found it's helpful to schedule an orientation a few weeks before the first board meeting of the fiscal year.

New board members have steep learning curves, and starting with an orientation early is a good way to help them get up to speed.

An orientation should be about 90 minutes. There should be time for the recent history of the organization and the board, a discussion of the big issues the board is looking at, time for the financials, and time for Q&A. It would be helpful to distribute copies of the most recent board packet so board members can see how information is presented and ask questions. Usually these meetings should be led by the president or president-elect, and the executive director.

## Mentorship

Some boards assign a "veteran" board member to be a mentor to the new board member to help the new member adjust. The mentor might take the new board member out for coffee after a couple of meeting to see how it's going. The mentor might be available for a phone call or emailed questions from the new member.

The process should be managed by the governance committee. It involves identifying mentors, setting expectations, and perhaps conducting an anonymous survey of the new board members at the end of the year to see how it went.

That said, I've seen more nonprofits talk about mentorship than actually implement a plan. So if it's one too many things for your committee and board, it's probably fine to it let go until you have more time to focus on it.

## Start over!

Now that it's a new fiscal year, it's time to start the whole process over again! Yes, looking for new board members might seem like a never-ending task. But as the quality of the board improves—thanks to the hard work of identifying, interviewing, and preparing new board members—you will find that overall quality of your applicant pool improves too. In other words, the job should get a little bit easier every year, until the hardest problem you have is choosing between too many great candidates.

## WAS THIS BOOK HELPFUL TO YOU?

Please considering leaving a review online to help other small
nonprofit managers find this resource as well!

———

### *Also by Erik Hanberg*

*The Little Book of Nonprofit Leadership: An Executive Director's
Handbook for Small (and Very Small) Nonprofits*

*The Little Book of Gold: Fundraising for Small (and Very Small)
Nonprofits*

*The Little Book of Likes: Social Media for Small (and Very Small)
Nonprofits*

# CONSULTING AND SPEAKING

I've traveled across the country facilitating board retreats and working with nonprofits of all sizes. I've also spoken at several nonprofit events and conferences about fundraising, nonprofit leaderships, marketing, boards, and much more.

If after reading this book or my others, you think I'd be a good fit for your nonprofit or association and want to learn more you can find more at ForSmallNonprofits.com.

You can also sign up here to receive more information from Erik Hanberg about all facets of small nonprofit management:
http://bit.ly/forsmallnonprofitsemail

# ABOUT THE AUTHOR

Erik Hanberg is an expert in nonprofit management, fundraising, marketing, and leadership. His books for nonprofits have sold more than 20,000 copies.

He has served as the director of two nonprofits, the interim executive director of two more, and served in positions in marketing and fundraising. He has been on more than twelve boards. In addition, he has consulted with nonprofit boards and staff of dozens and dozens of nonprofits and foundations across the country.

He has served for 12 years as an elected official on the Metro Parks Board of Tacoma, a junior municipality with an annual operating budget of $50+ million.

He lives in Tacoma, Washington, with his wife and two children. In addition to his nonprofit writing, he also has several novels, and even a play or two.

———

Find him online at:
  https://www.forsmallnonprofits.com
  https://www.erikhanberg.com
  or on Twitter at @erikhanberg.

The Little Book of Boards
A Board Member's Handbook for Small (and Very Small) Nonprofits
Published by Side x Side Publishing
Copyright © Erik Hanberg 2015

Cover Design by Mary Holste

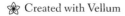 Created with Vellum

Made in the USA
Coppell, TX
13 January 2022

71530854R00111